EASY PIANO

ACOUSTIC *classics*

2	**American Pie**	Don McLean
12	**Angie**	The Rolling Stones
17	**Babe, I'm Gonna Leave You**	Led Zeppelin
24	**Baby, I Love Your Way**	Peter Frampton
34	**Behind Blue Eyes**	The Who
40	**Best of My Love**	Eagles
46	**Dust in the Wind**	Kansas
29	**Free Fallin'**	Tom Petty & The Heartbreakers
52	**Give a Little Bit**	Supertramp
49	**Here Comes the Sun**	The Beatles
57	**I'd Love to Change the World**	Ten Years After
62	**Landslide**	Fleetwood Mac
70	**Leaving on a Jet Plane**	Peter, Paul & Mary
84	**Longer**	Dan Fogelberg
90	**More Than Words**	Extreme
73	**Night Moves**	Bob Seger
96	**Norwegian Wood (This Bird Has Flown)**	The Beatles
99	**Seven Bridges Road**	Eagles
106	**Suite: Judy Blue Eyes**	Crosby, Stills & Nash
118	**Take Me Home, Country Roads**	John Denver
126	**Tears in Heaven**	Eric Clapton
121	**Time in a Bottle**	Jim Croce
130	**Wanted Dead or Alive**	Bon Jovi
142	**Yesterday**	The Beatles
137	**You've Got a Friend**	James Taylor

ISBN 0-634-09261-8

HAL•LEONARD®
CORPORATION

7777 W. BLUEMOUND RD. P.O. BOX 13819 MILWAUKEE, WI 53213

Visit Hal Leonard Online at
www.halleonard.com

AMERICAN PIE

Words and Music by
DON McLEAN

Freely, not fast

A long, long time a-go, I can still re-

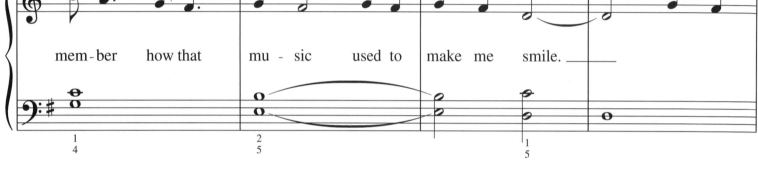

mem-ber how that mu-sic used to make me smile.

And I knew if I had my chance that

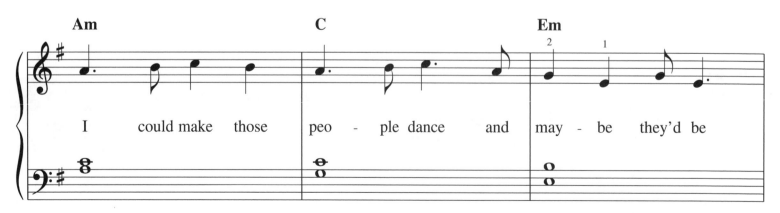

I could make those peo-ple dance and may-be they'd be

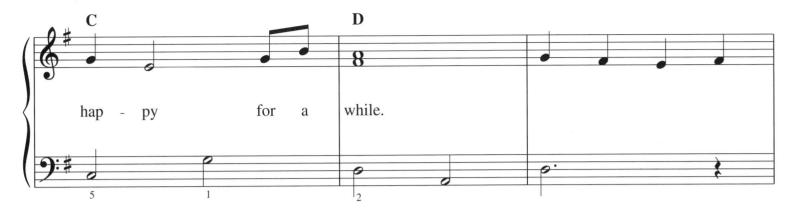

hap - py   for   a   while.

But Feb - ru - ar - y   made me shiv - er   with ev - 'ry pa - per

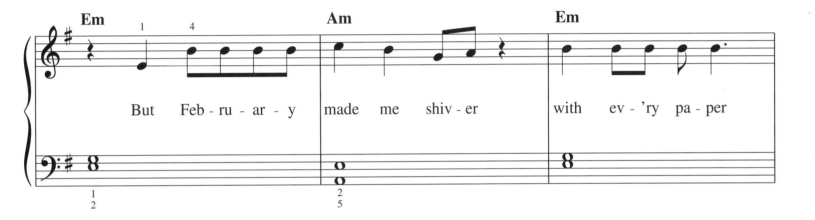

I'd   de - liv - er.   Bad news   on   the   door - step,   I

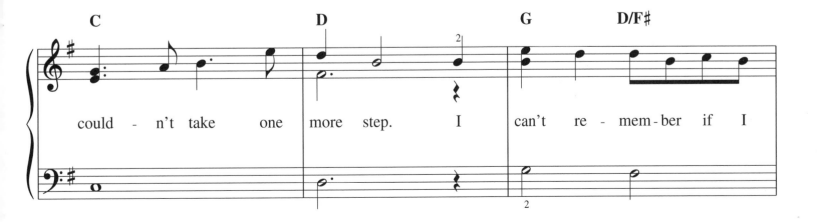

could - n't take   one   more step.   I   can't re - mem - ber if I

cried   when I   read   a - bout ___ his   wid - owed   bride.

Some - thing touched me   deep   in - side _____ the   day   the   mu - sic

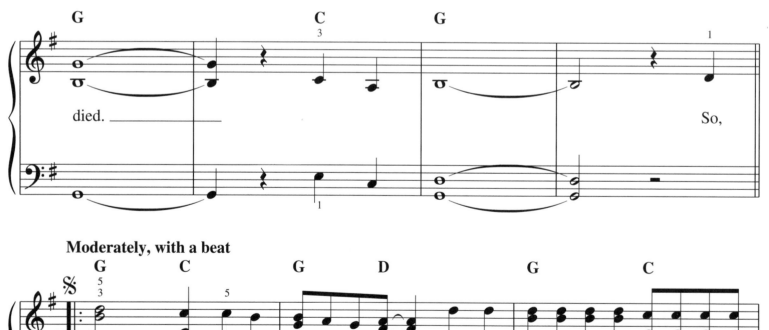

died. _____   So,

Moderately, with a beat

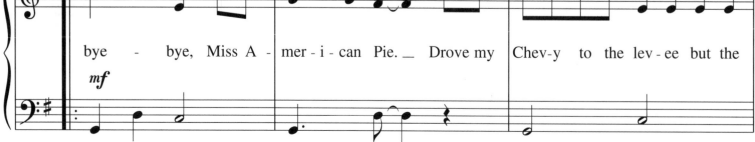

bye - bye, Miss A - mer - i - can Pie. __ Drove my   Chev - y   to the lev - ee   but the

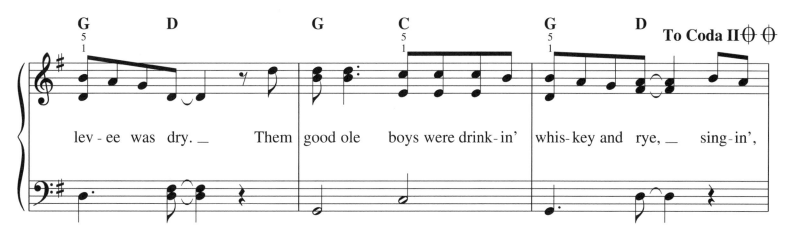

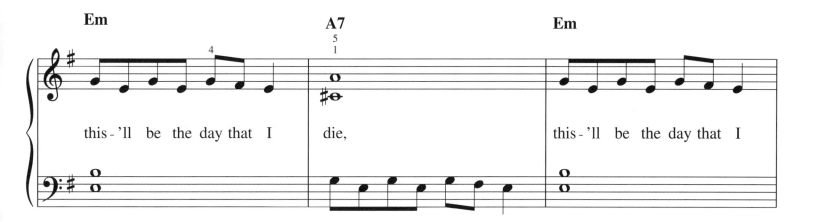

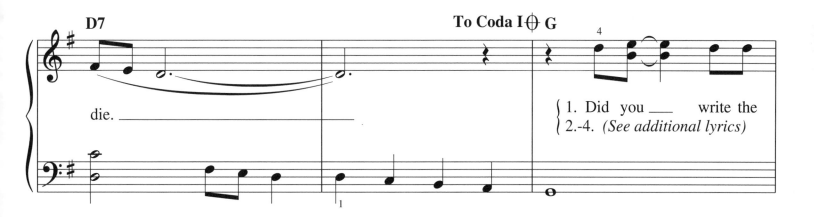

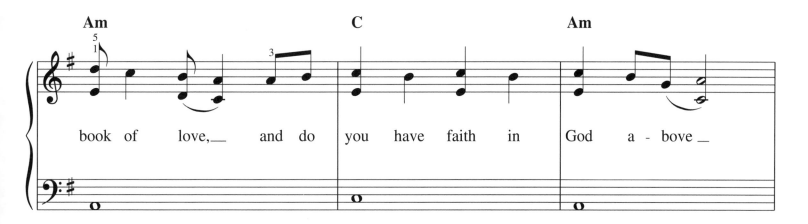

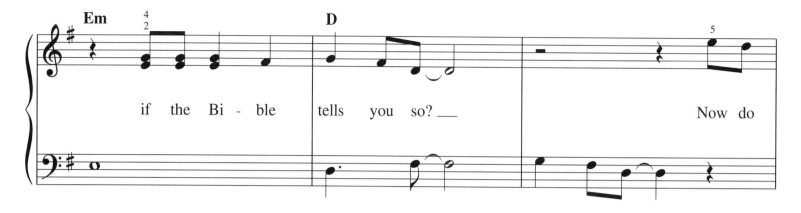

if the Bi - ble tells you so? ___ Now do

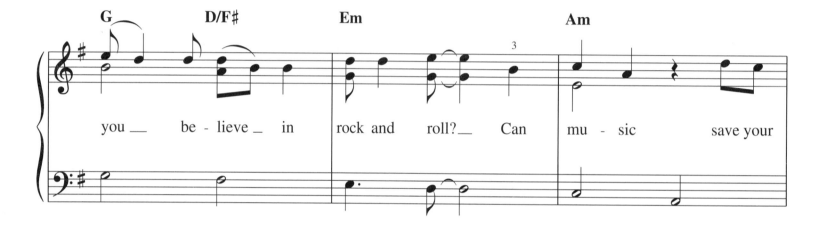

you ___ be - lieve ___ in rock and roll? ___ Can mu - sic save your

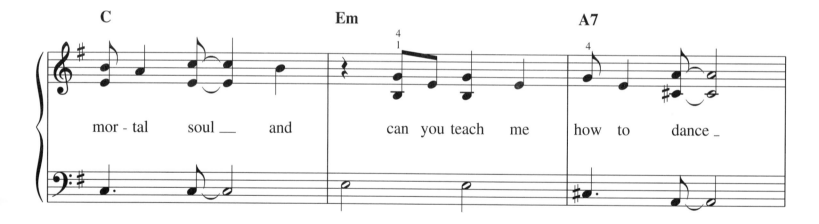

mor - tal soul ___ and can you teach me how to dance ___

real slow? ___ Well, I know that you're ___ in

love   with   him __ 'cause I ____   saw you danc - in'   in   the   gym, __   you

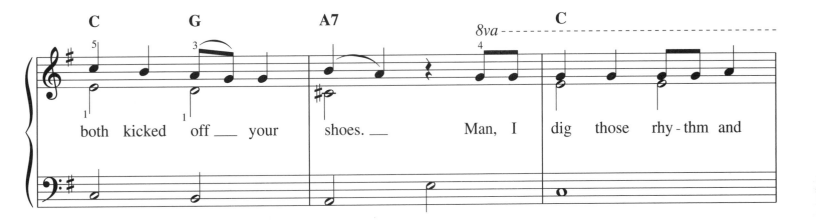

both   kicked   off __ your   shoes. __   Man, I   dig   those   rhy - thm and

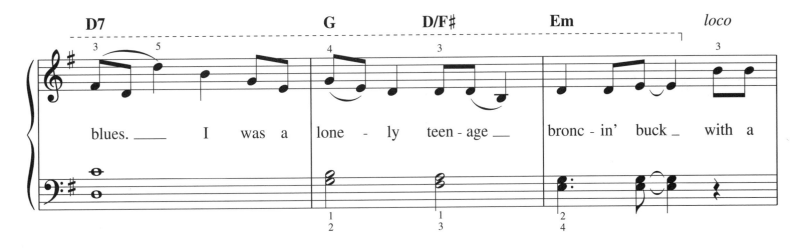

blues. ____   I   was a   lone - ly   teen - age __   bronc - in'   buck __   with a

pink   car - na - tion and a   pick - up   truck. __ But   I   knew I ____   was

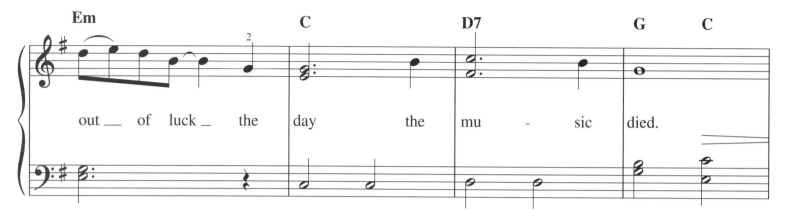

out __ of luck __ the day the mu - sic died.

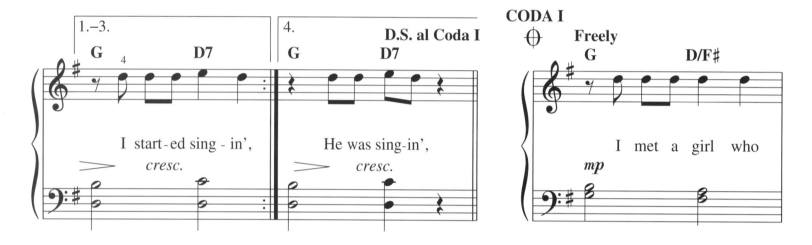

1.–3.
I start-ed sing - in',
cresc.

4.
He was sing-in',
cresc.

D.S. al Coda I

CODA I

Freely
I met a girl who
mp

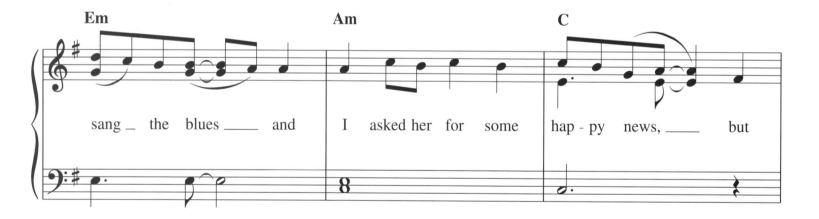

sang __ the blues _____ and I asked her for some hap - py news, _____ but

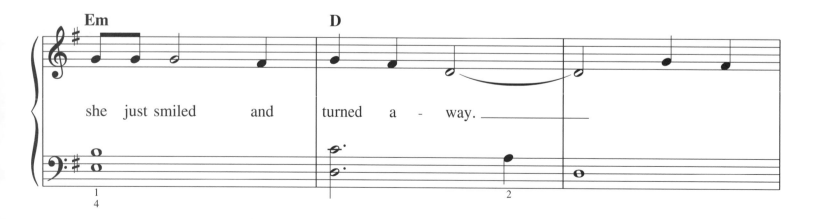

she just smiled and turned a - way. _____

I went down to the sa-cred store _____ where I

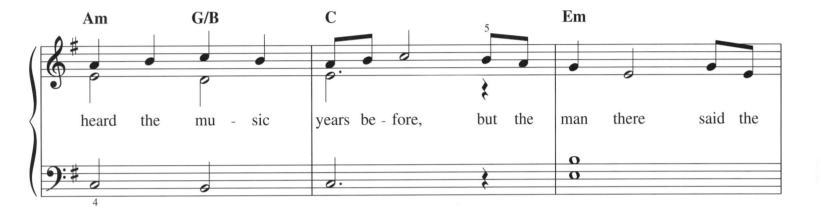

heard the mu - sic years be-fore, but the man there said the

mu - sic would-n't play. _____ And

in the streets the chil - dren screamed, the lov - ers cried and the

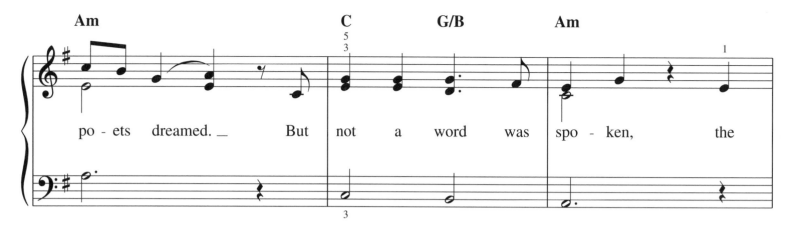

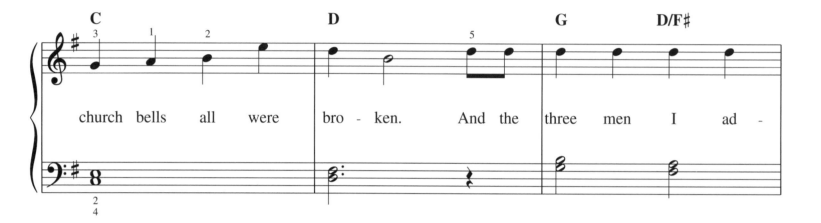

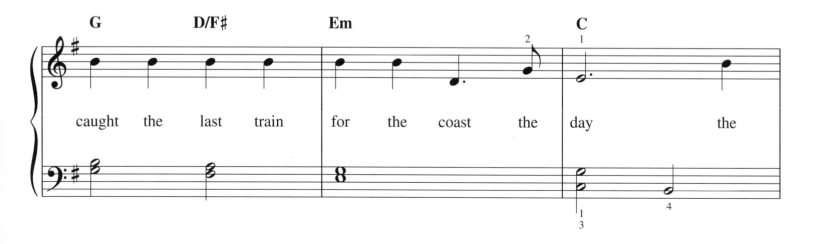

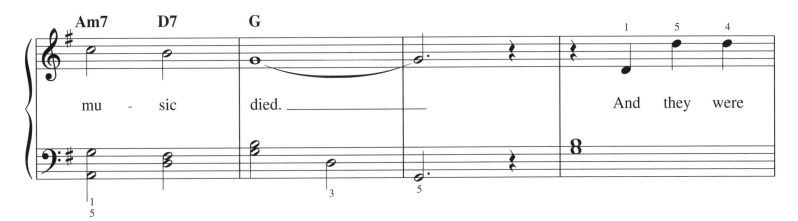

mu - sic   died. _____   And they were

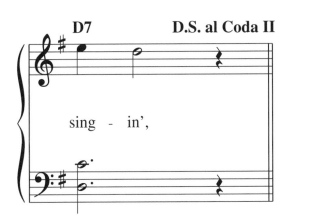

sing - in',

CODA II

this - 'll be the day that I   die.

rit.

Additional Lyrics

2. Now for ten years we've been on our own,
   And moss grows fat on a rollin' stone
   But that's not how it used to be
   When the jester sang for the king and queen
   In a coat he borrowed from James Dean
   And a voice that came from you and me
   Oh and while the king was looking down,
   The jester stole his thorny crown
   The courtroom was adjourned,
   No verdict was returned
   And while Lenin read a book on Marx
   The quartet practiced in the park
   And we sang dirges in the dark
   The day the music died
   We were singin'... bye-bye... etc.

3. Helter-skelter in the summer swelter
   The birds flew off with a fallout shelter
   Eight miles high and fallin' fast,
   It landed foul on the grass
   The players tried for a forward pass,
   With the jester on the sidelines in a cast
   Now the half-time air was sweet perfume
   While the sergeants played a marching tune
   We all got up to dance
   But we never got the chance
   'Cause the players tried to take the field,
   The marching band refused to yield
   Do you recall what was revealed
   The day the music died
   We started singin'... bye-bye... etc.

4. And there we were all in one place,
   A generation lost in space
   With no time left to start again
   So come on, Jack be nimble, Jack be quick
   Jack Flash sat on a candlestick
   'Cause fire is the devil's only friend
   And as I watched him on the stage
   My hands were clenched in fists of rage
   No angel born in hell
   Could break that Satan's spell
   And as the flames climbed high into the night
   To light the sacrificial rite
   I saw Satan laughing with delight
   The day the music died
   He was singin'... bye-bye... etc.

ANGIE

Words and Music by MICK JAGGER
and KEITH RICHARDS

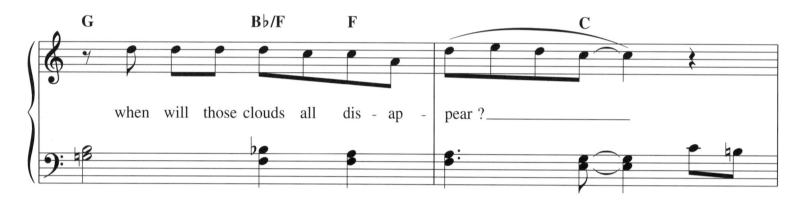

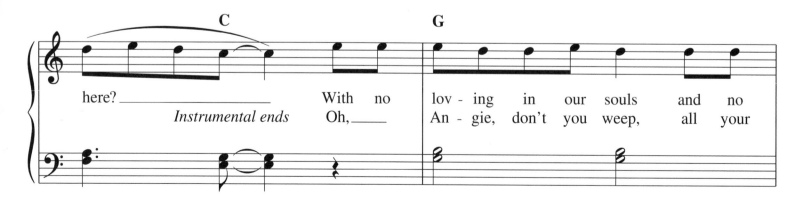

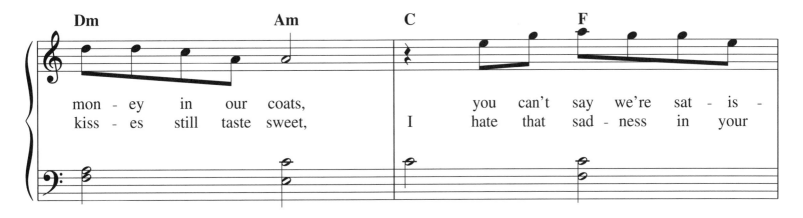

mon - ey in our coats,
kiss - es still taste sweet,

you can't say we're sat - is -
hate that sad - ness in your

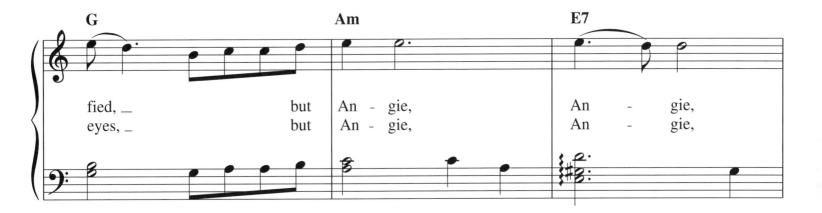

fied, __ but An - gie,
eyes, __ but An - gie,

An - gie,
An - gie,

you can't say we nev - er tried. _____
ain't it time we said good - bye? _____ (Oh,

To Coda ⊕

An - gie, you're beau - ti - ful,
yes.) *Instrumental*

but ain't it time we said good-

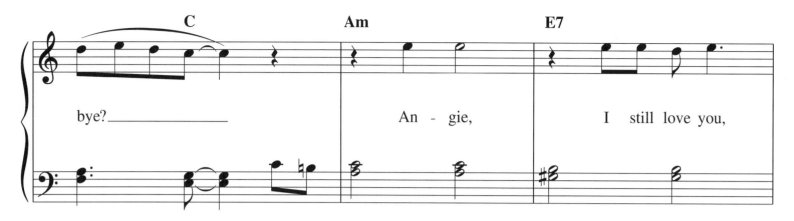

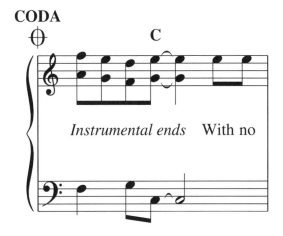

D.S. al Coda

CODA

where will it lead us from here?" _____

Instrumental ends With no

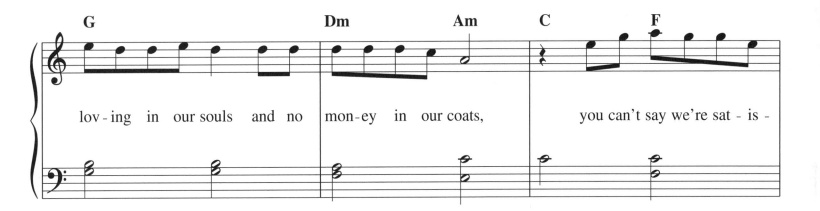

lov-ing in our souls and no mon-ey in our coats, you can't say we're sat - is -

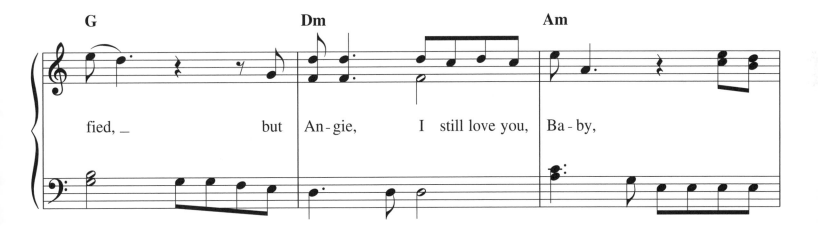

fied, _ but An-gie, I still love you, Ba-by,

ev-'ry-where I look I see your eyes. _____

Dm   Am   C   F

There ain't a wom-an that comes close to you,   come on, Ba-by, dry your

G   Am   E7

eyes._____   But An-gie,   An - gie,

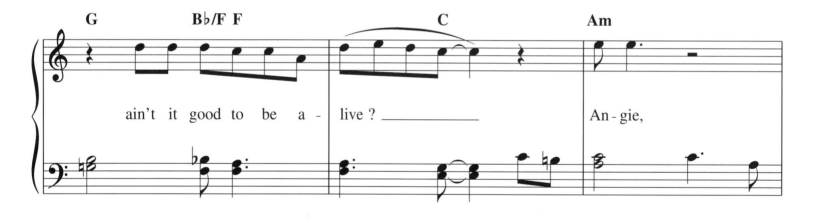

G   Bb/F F   C   Am

ain't it good to be a - live? _____   An-gie,

E7   G   Bb/F F   C

An - gie,   they can't say we nev - er   tried._____

BABE, I'M GONNA LEAVE YOU

Words and Music by ANNE BREDON,
JIMMY PAGE and ROBERT PLANT

With motion, not too slow

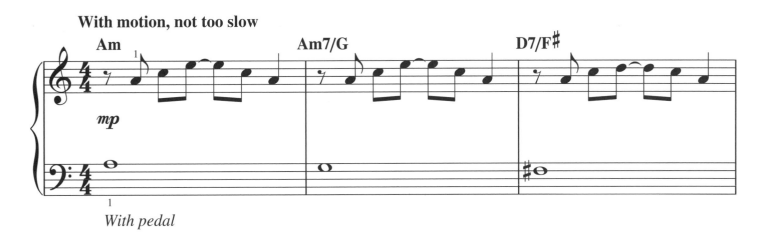

With pedal

Babe,_____

_____ ba - by, ba - by, I'm gon - na

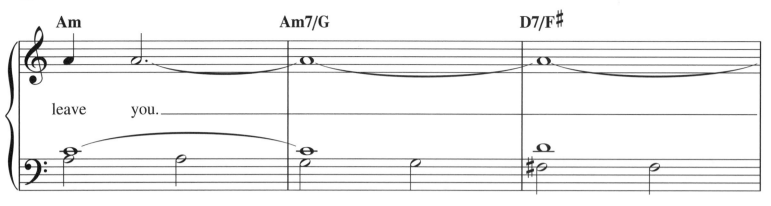

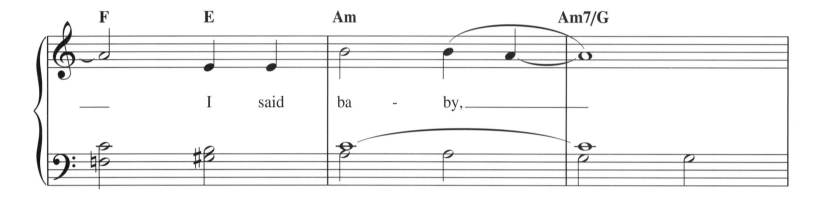

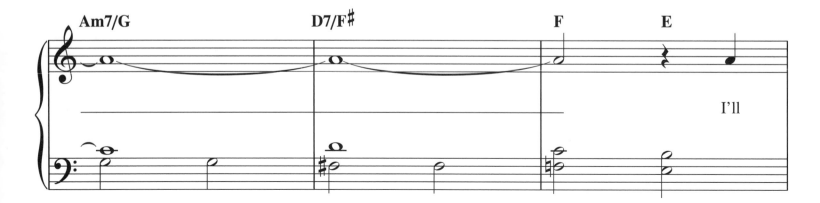

leave you when the sum - mer - time,____ leave you when the

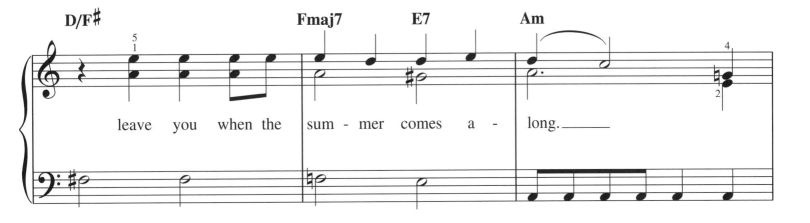

sum - mer comes a - roll - in',____

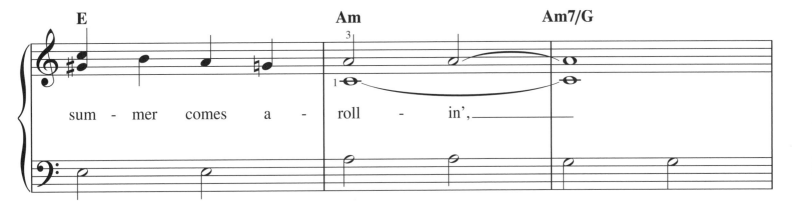

leave you when the sum - mer comes a - long.____

20

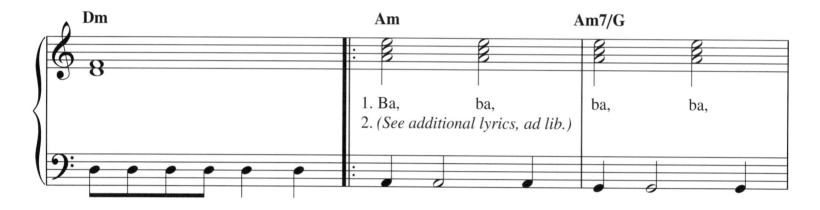

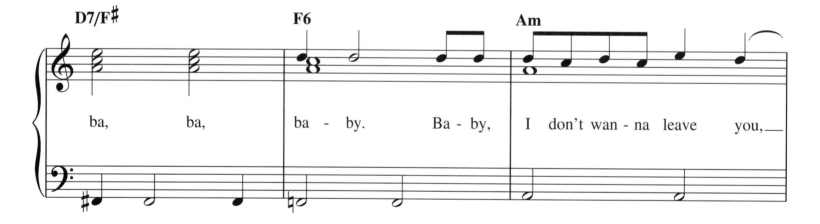

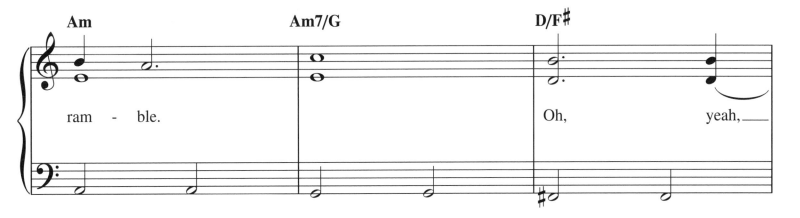

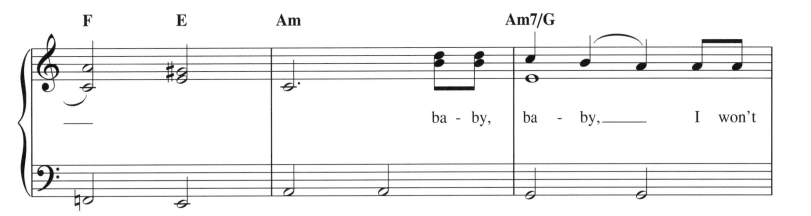

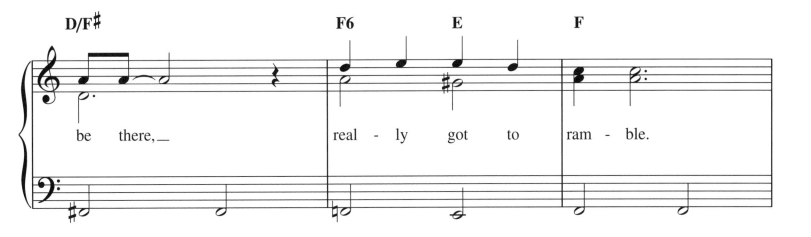

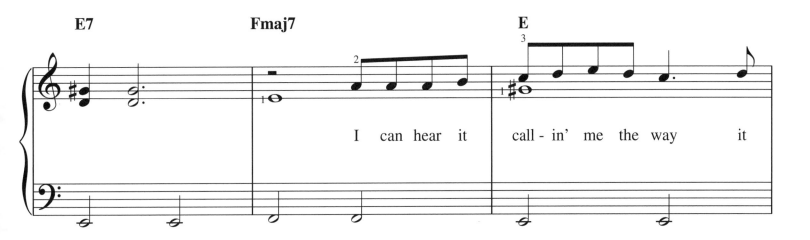

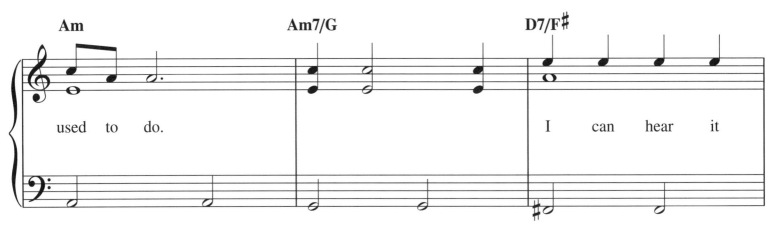

used to do. I can hear it

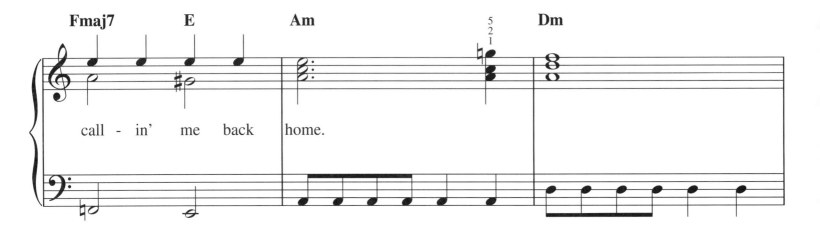

call - in' me back home.

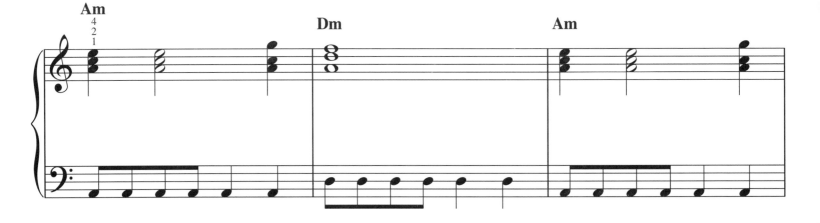

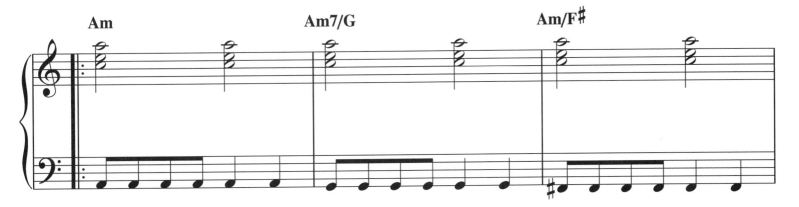

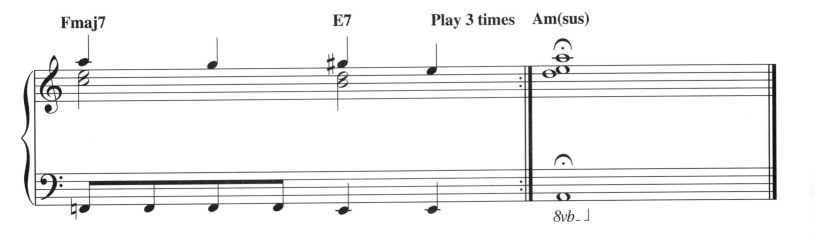

Additional Lyrics

I know, I know, I know, I never, I never, I never, I never, I never leave you, baby.
But I got to go away from this place, I've got to quit you.
Ooh, baby, baby, baby, baby
Baby, baby, baby, ooh don't you hear it callin'?
Woman, woman, I know, I know it's good to have you back again
And I know that one day baby, it's really gonna grow, yes it is.
We gonna go walkin' through the park every day.
Hear what I say, every day.
Baby, it's really growin', you made me happy when skies were grey.
But now I've got to go away.
Baby, baby, baby, baby
That's when it's callin' me
That's when it's callin' me back home...

BABY, I LOVE YOUR WAY

Words and Music by
PETER FRAMPTON

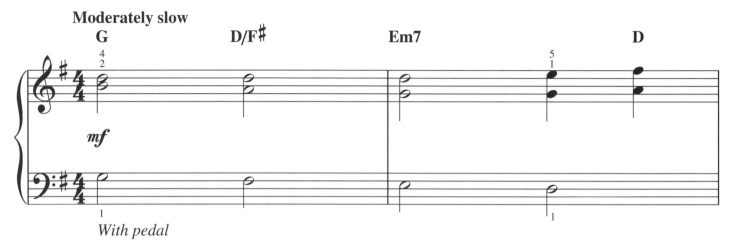

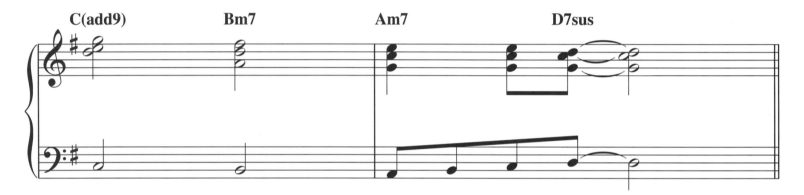

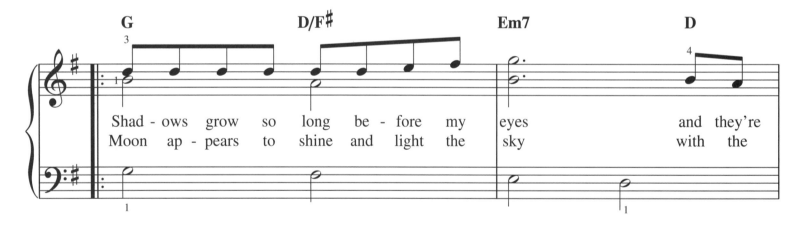

Shad - ows grow so long be - fore my eyes and they're
Moon ap - pears to shine and light the sky with the

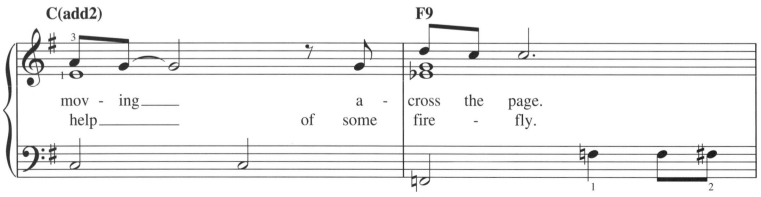

mov - ing___ a - cross the page.
help___ of some fire - fly.

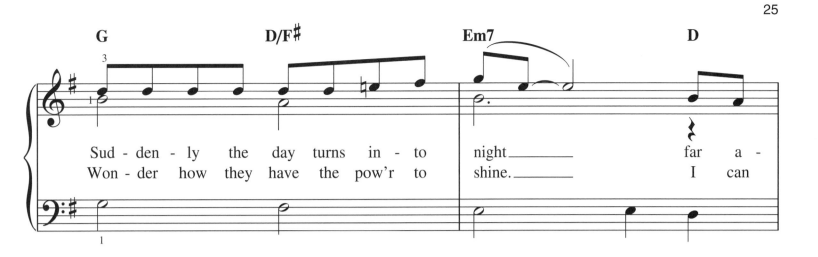

Sud - den - ly the day turns in - to night_____ far a -
Won - der how they have the pow'r to shine._____ I can

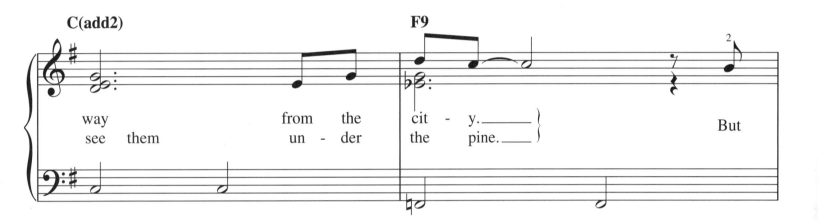

way from the cit - y._____ But
see them un - der the pine._____

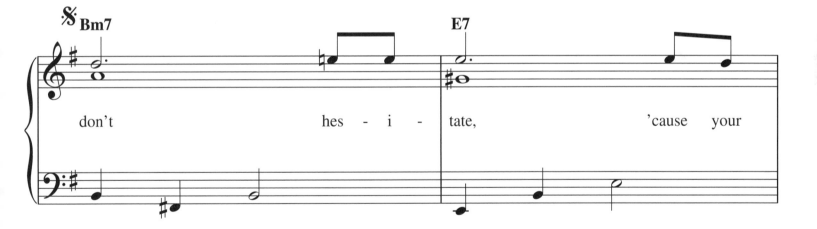

don't hes - i - tate, 'cause your

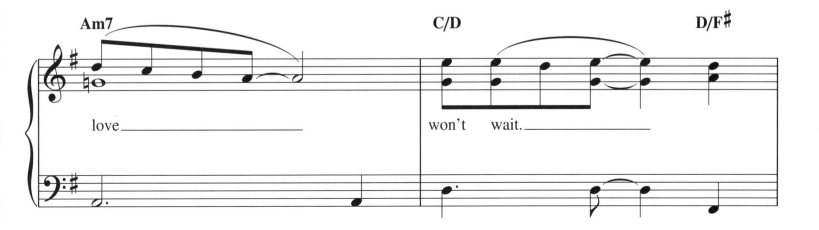

love_____ won't wait.

G   **D**   **Am7**   **C**

Ooh, ba - by, I love your way___ ev -'ry day.___

G   **D**   **Am7**   **C**

Wan - na tell you I love your way___ ev -'ry day.___

G   **D**   **Am7**   **C**   **To Coda**

Wan - na be with you night and day.___

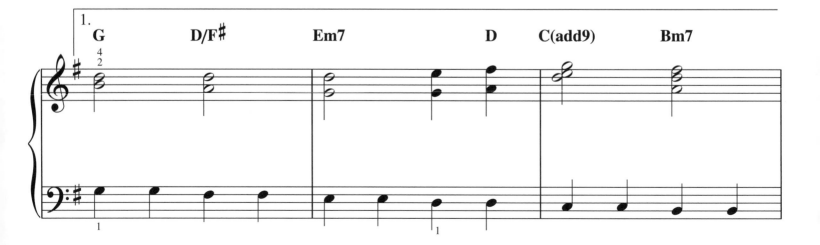

1.

G   **D/F♯**   **Em7**   **D**   **C(add9)**   **Bm7**

27

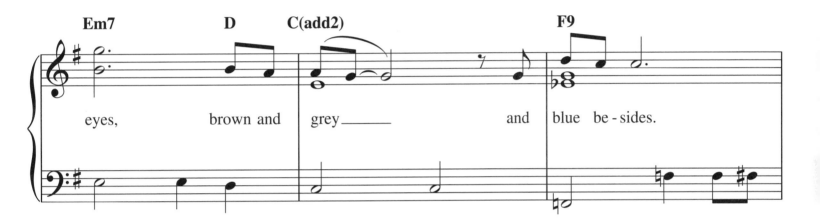

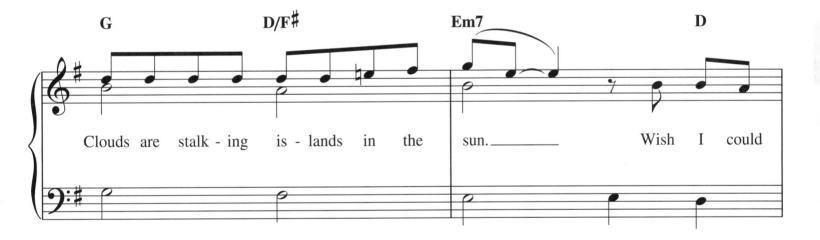

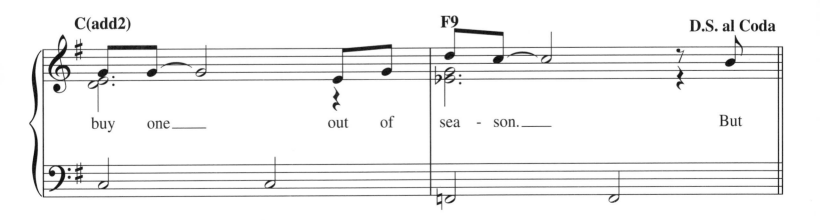

Ooh, ba - by, I love your way___ ev - 'ry day.___

Wan - na tell you I love your way.___ Ooh.___

Wan - na be with you night and day.

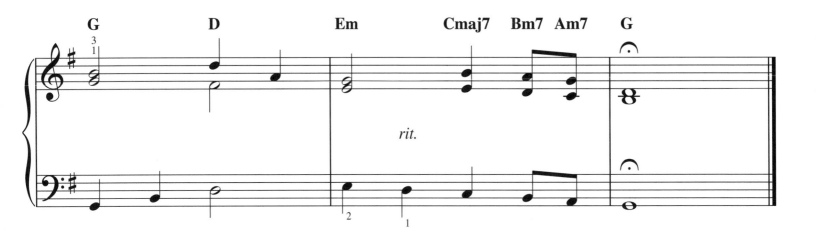

rit.

FREE FALLIN'

Words and Music by TOM PETTY
and JEFF LYNNE

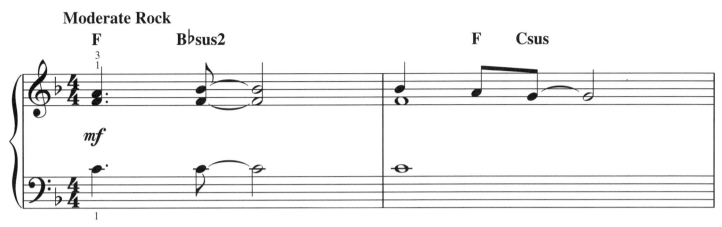

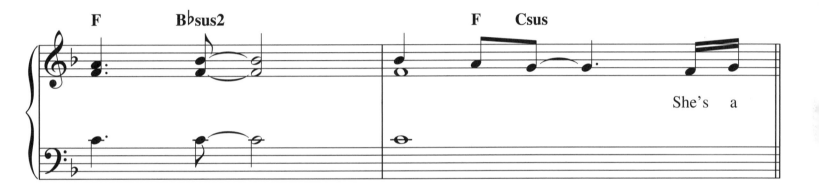

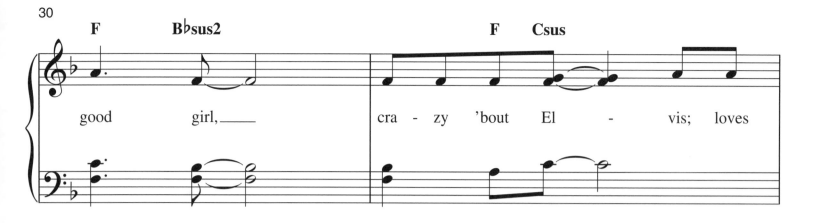

good girl,_____ cra - zy 'bout El - vis; loves

hors - es_____ and her boy - friend too._____

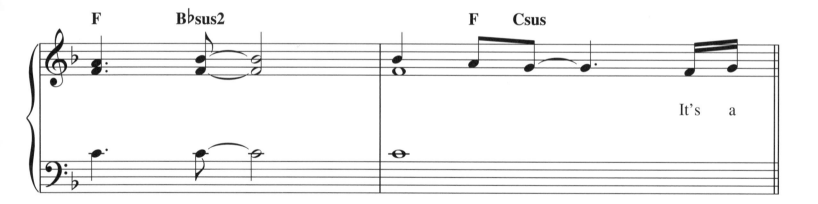

It's a

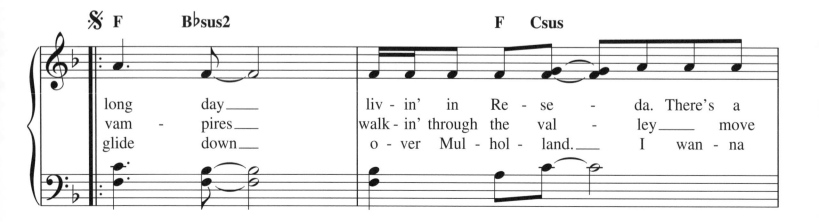

long day_____ liv - in' in Re - se - da. There's a
vam - pires_____ walk - in' through the val - ley_____ move
glide down_____ o - ver Mul - hol - land.____ I wan - na

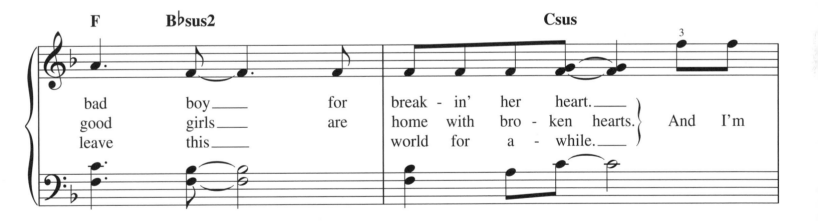

Yeah, I'm free, free

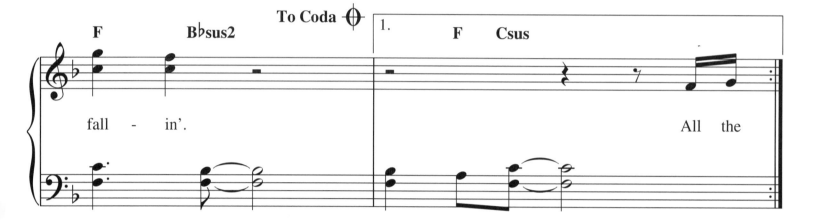

fall - in'. All the

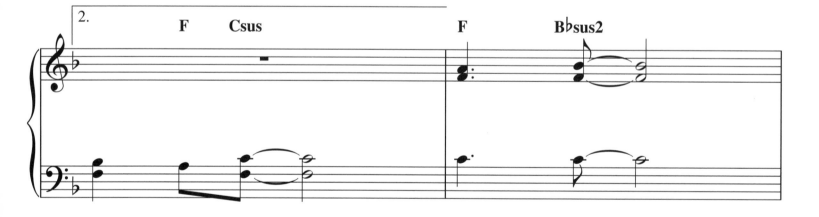

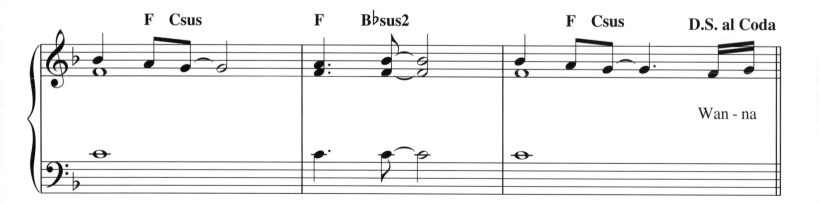

Wan - na

BEHIND BLUE EYES

Words and Music by
PETE TOWNSHEND

No one knows what it's like to be the bad man,
No one knows what it's like to feel these feel - ings

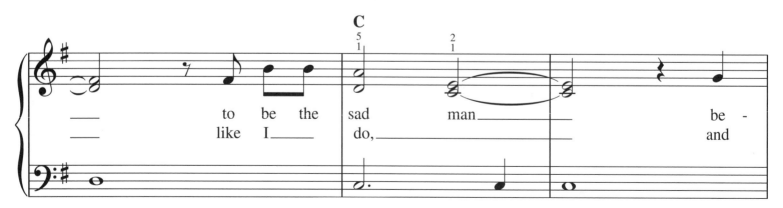

to be the sad man like I do,
like I do, and be -

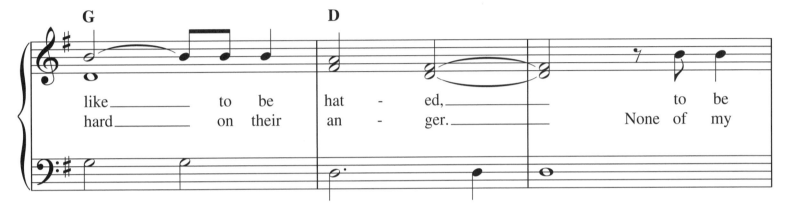

emp - ty _____ as my con - science

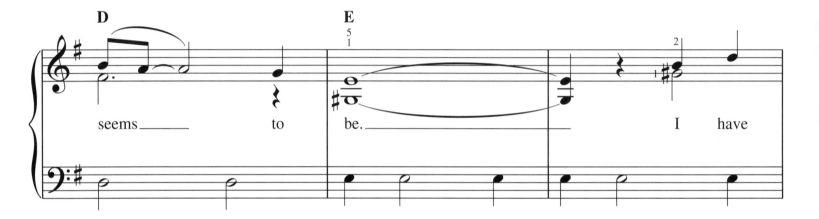

seems _____ to be. _____ I have

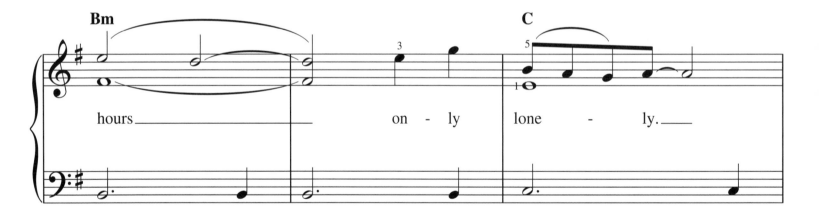

hours _____ on - ly lone - ly. ___

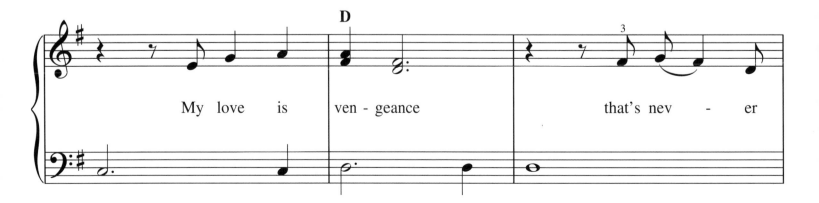

My love is ven - geance that's nev - er

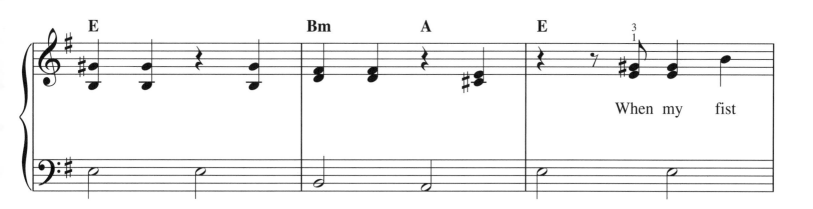

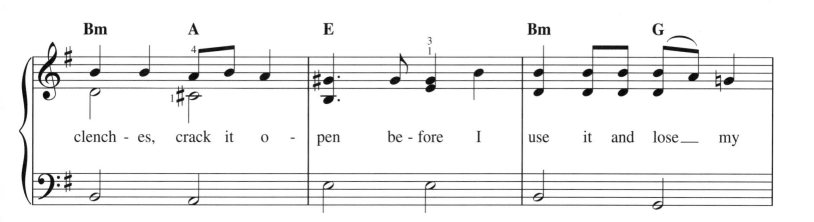

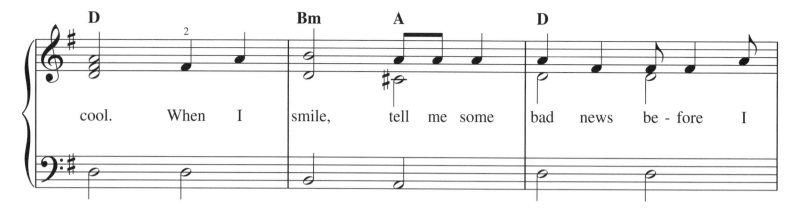

cool. When I   smile,   tell me some   bad news be - fore I

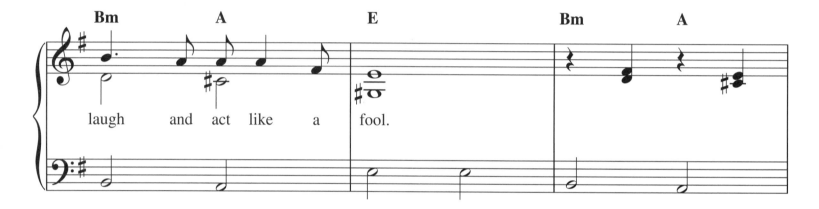

laugh   and act like a   fool.

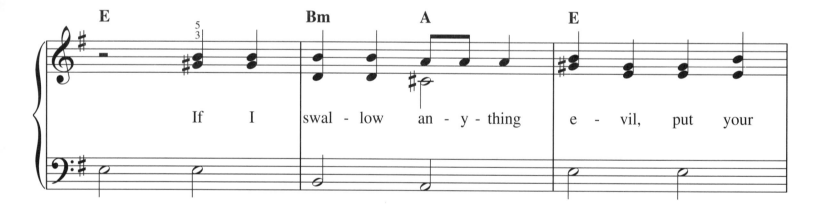

If I   swal - low an - y - thing   e - vil, put your

fin - ger down_ my   throat. And if I   shiv - er, please give me a

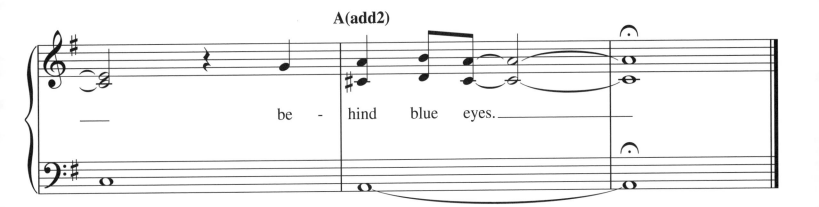

BEST OF MY LOVE

Words and Music by JOHN DAVID SOUTHER,
DON HENLEY and GLENN FREY

Moderately slow

Ev - er - y night___ I'm ly - in' in bed,___
Beau - ti - ful fac - es and loud emp - ty plac - es,

hold - in' you close___ in my dreams;___
look at the way___ that we live;___

think - in' a - bout___ all the things that we said_____ and
wast - in' our time____ on cheap talk and wine_____

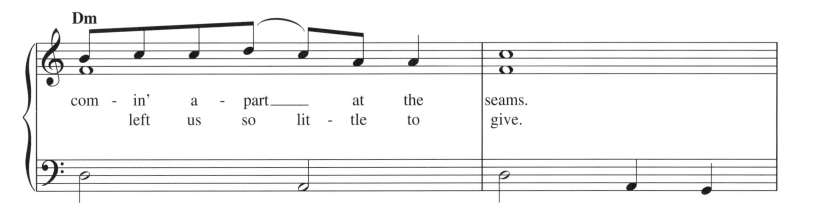

com - in' a - part____ at the seams.
left us so lit - tle to give.

We try to talk it o - ver_____ but the
That same old crowd was like a cold dark cloud that

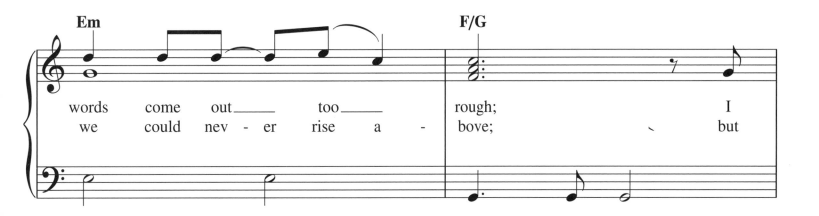

words come out____ too____ rough; I
we could nev - er rise a - bove; but

know you were try - in' to give me the best____ of your
here in my heart I give you the best____ of my

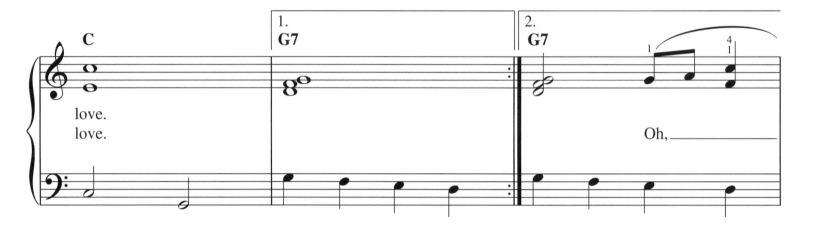

1. **G7**

2. **G7**

love.
love. Oh,_____

____ sweet dar - lin',____ you get the best of my

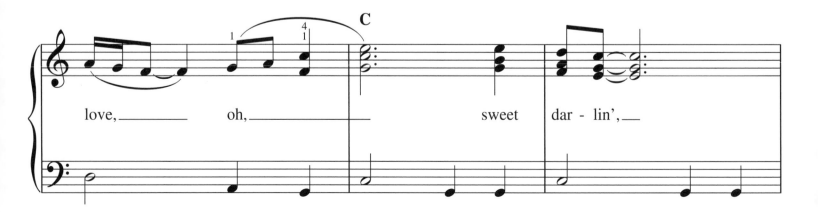

love,_____ oh,_____ ____ sweet dar - lin',____

Dm   **Fm7**

you get the best of my   love.   I'm go - in'

                                    C

back in time____ and it's a   sweet____ dream;____   it was a

Fm7

qui - et night____ and I would   be all____ right____ if I could

Dm7   **G7**   **C**

go____ on   sleep - ing. But ev - 'ry morn - in' I

wake up and wor — — ry   what's gon - na hap-pen to - day;___

you see it your___ way, and   I see it mine,___ but we

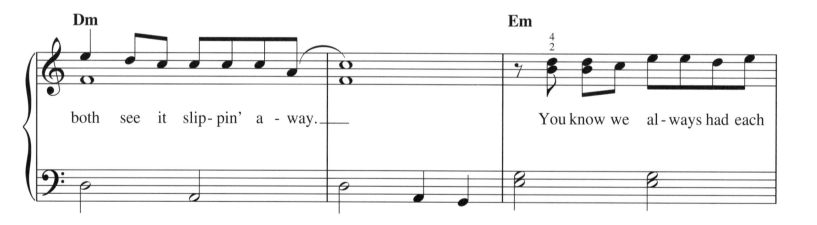

both see it slip-pin' a - way.___   You know we al-ways had each

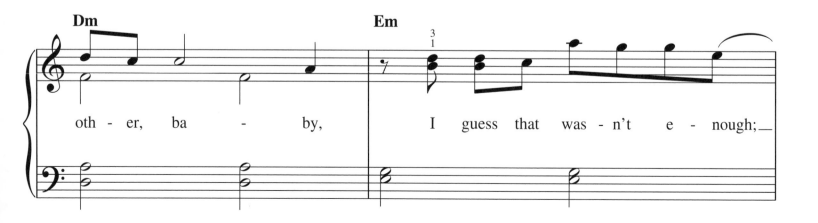

oth - er, ba — — by,   I guess that was - n't e - nough;___

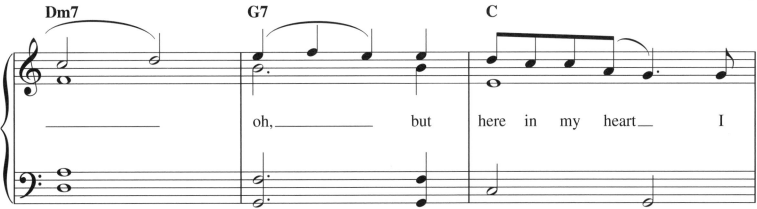

oh,_____ but here in my heart__ I

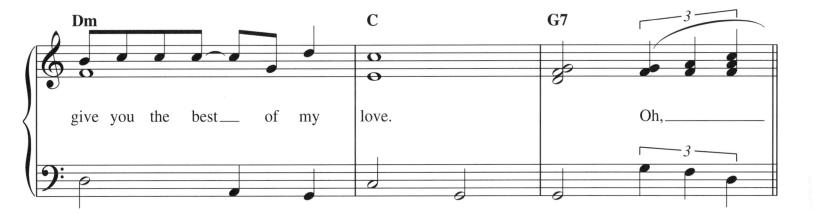

give you the best__ of my love.

Oh,_____

__ sweet dar - lin',__ you get the best of my

love._____ Oh,_____ love._____ Oh._____

DUST IN THE WIND

Words and Music by
KERRY LIVGREN

Moderate Folk style

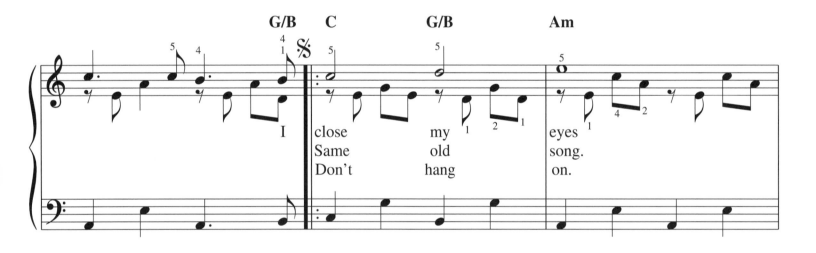

I close my eyes
Same old song.
Don't hang on.

on - ly for a mo-ment and the mo-ment's gone. All my
Just a drop of wa - ter in an end - less sea. All we
Noth-ing lasts for - ev - er but the earth and sky. It slips a -

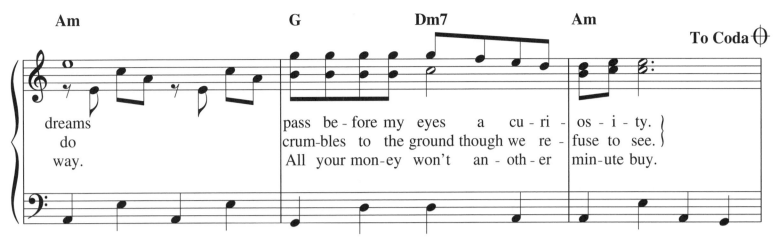

To Coda

dreams
do
way.

pass be - fore my eyes   a   cu - ri - os - i - ty.
crum-bles to the ground though we   re - fuse to see.
All your mon-ey won't   an - oth - er   min-ute buy.

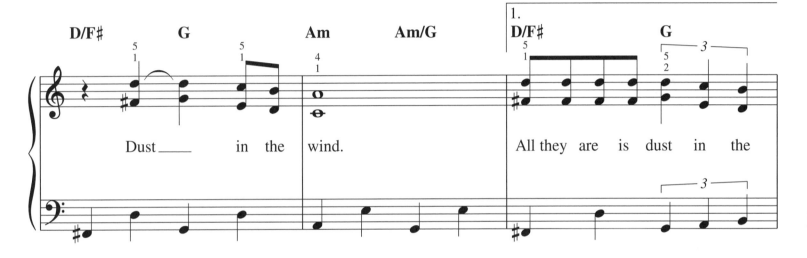

Dust _____ in the wind.

All they are is dust in the

wind.

All we are is dust in the   wind.

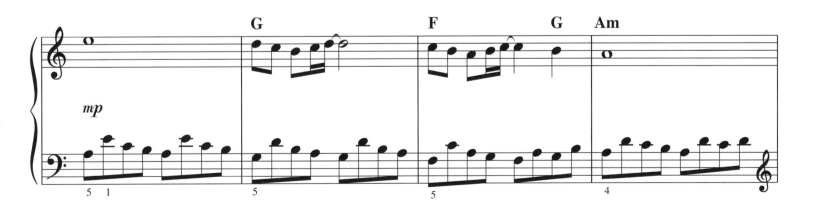

mp

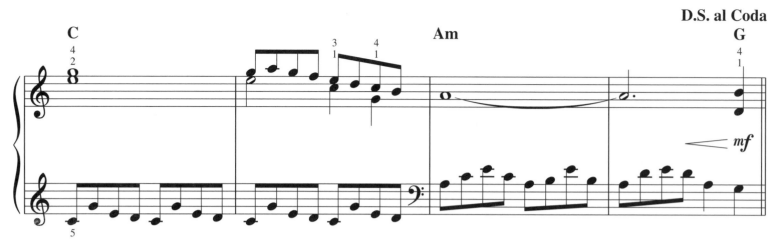

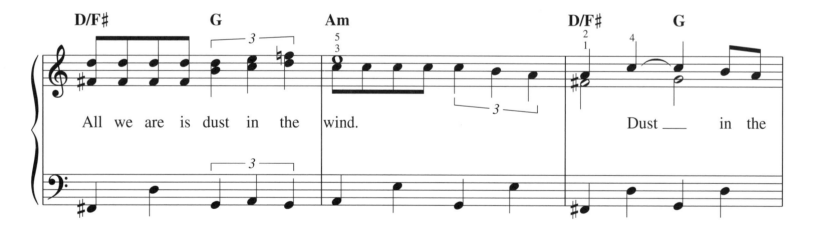

HERE COMES THE SUN

Words and Music by
GEORGE HARRISON

Moderately

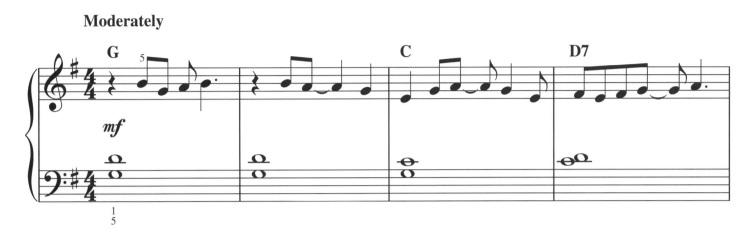

Here comes_ the sun, doo da doo doo. Here comes_ the

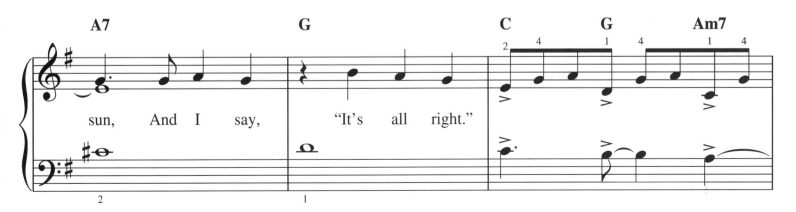

sun, And I say, "It's all right."

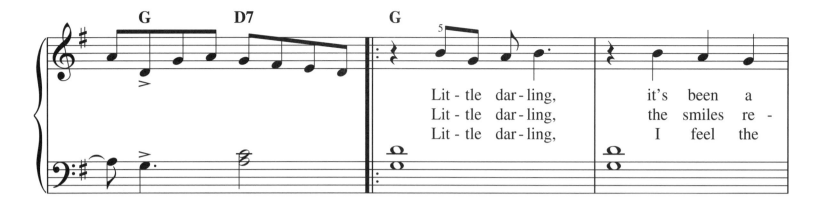

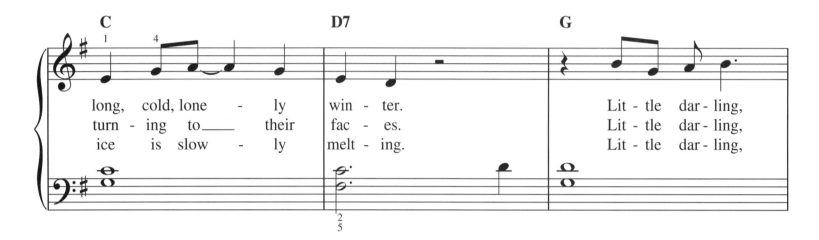

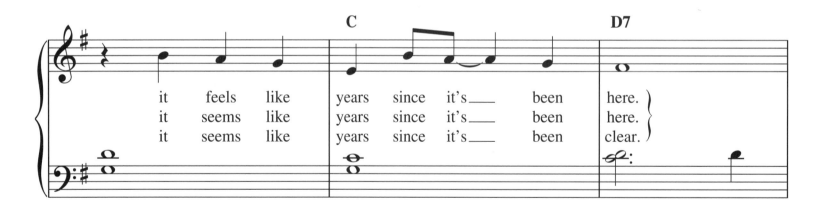

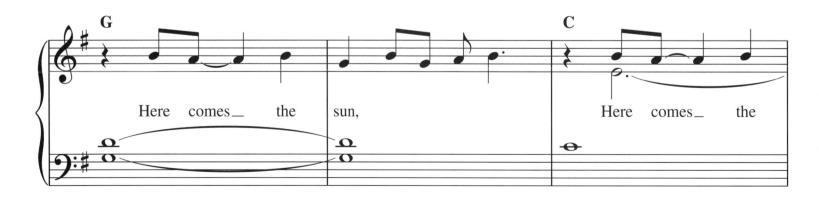

sun,   and I   say,   "It's   all   right."

"It's   all   right."

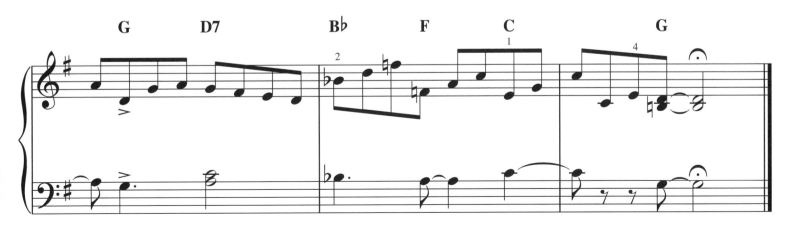

GIVE A LITTLE BIT

Words and Music by RICK DAVIES
and ROGER HODGSON

Moderate Rock

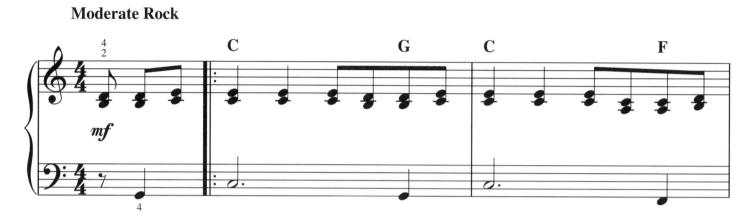

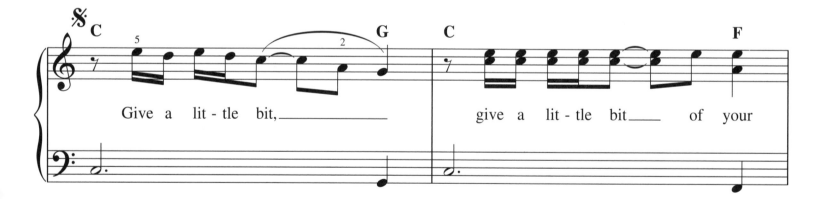

Give a lit-tle bit,_____ give a lit-tle bit___ of your

love to me. I'll give a lit-tle bit,_____

I'll give a lit-tle bit___ of my { love to you. / life for you.

There's so much___ that we need to share,___ so
Now the time___ that we need to share,___ so

To Coda ⊕

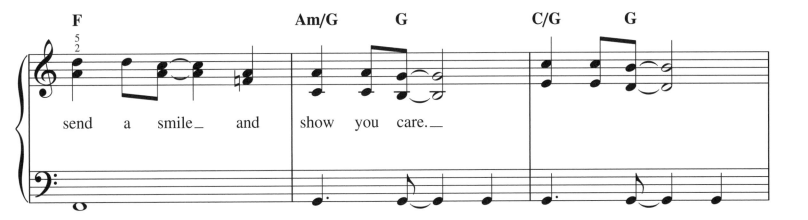

send a smile_ and show you care._

I'll give a lit-tle bit,_____ I'll give a lit-tle bit___ of my

life for you. So give a lit-tle bit,_____

oh, give a lit-tle bit____ of your time to me.

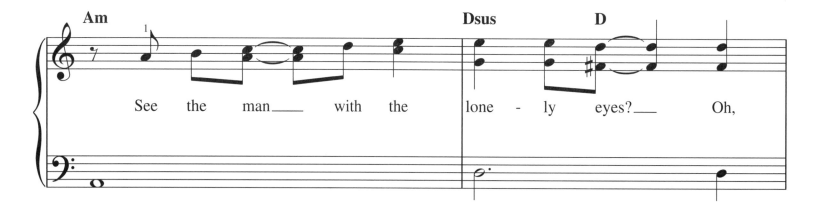

See the man____ with the lone - ly eyes?____ Oh,

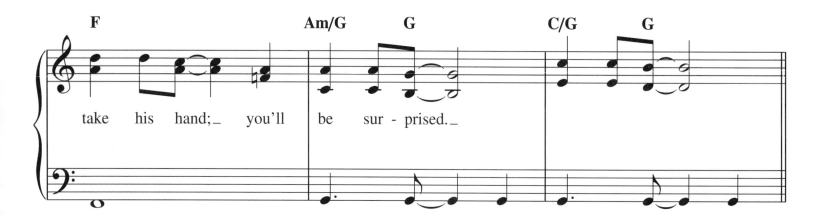

take his hand;_ you'll be sur - prised._

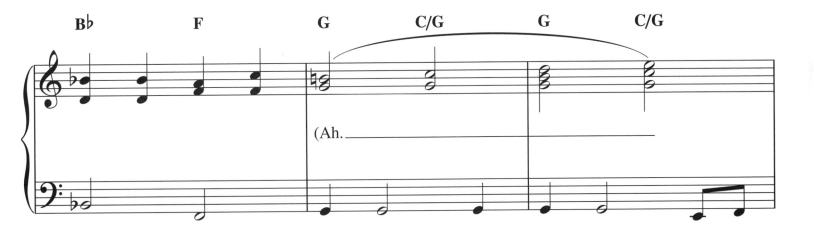

D.S. al Coda

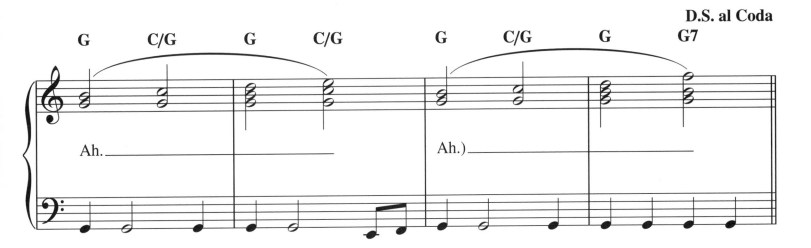

find your - self;___ we're on our way___ back

home. Oh, go - in' home.

Don't you need, don't you need to feel at home?

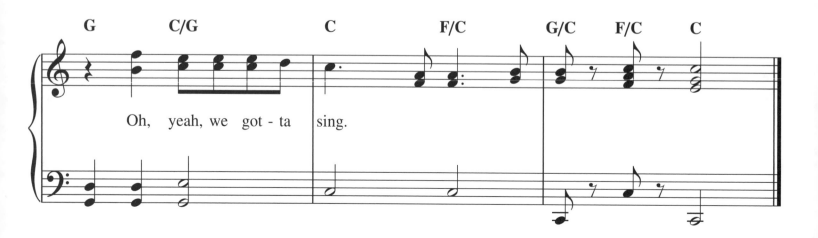

Oh, yeah, we got - ta sing.

I'D LOVE TO CHANGE THE WORLD

Words and Music by
ALVIN LEE

Moderately

With pedal

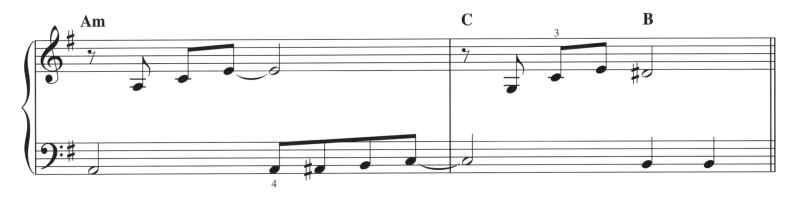

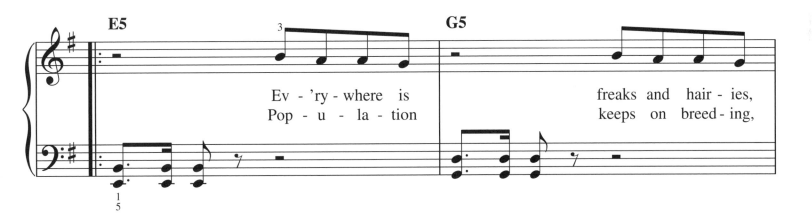

Ev - 'ry - where is / Pop - u - la - tion   freaks and hair - ies, / keeps on breed - ing,

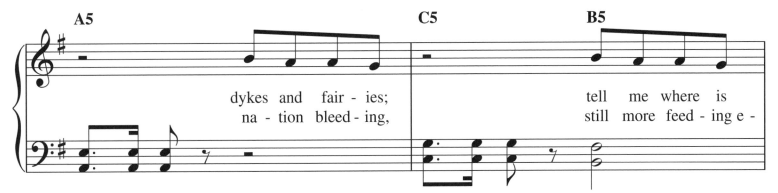

dykes and fair - ies; / na - tion bleed - ing,   tell me where is / still more feed - ing e -

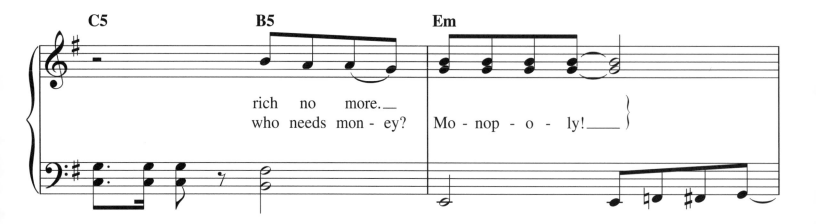

I'd

love to change the world,_____ but I don't_____

____ know what to do,

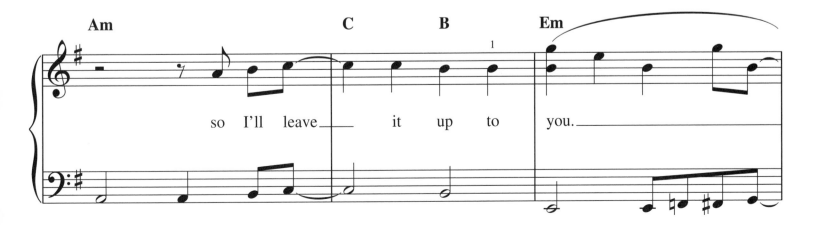

so I'll leave____ it up to you._____

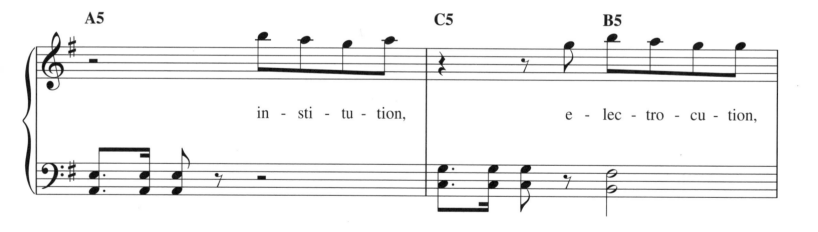

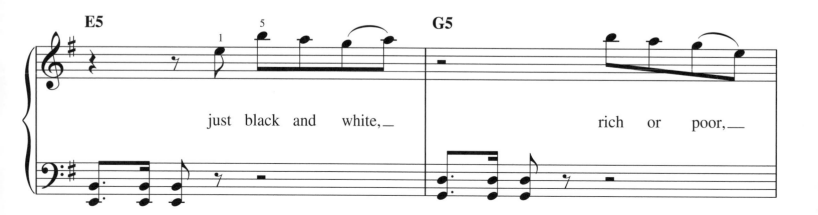

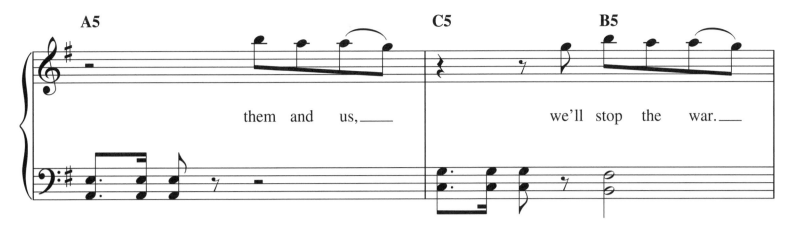

them and us,_____ we'll stop the war.____

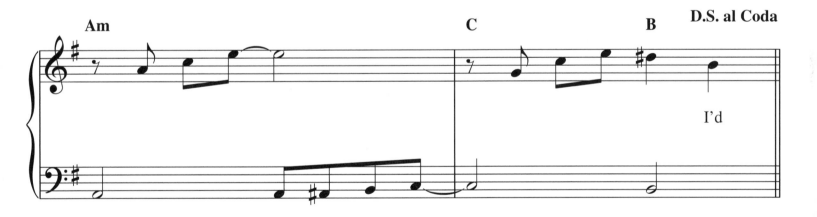

I'd

LANDSLIDE

Words and Music by
STEVIE NICKS

Moderately

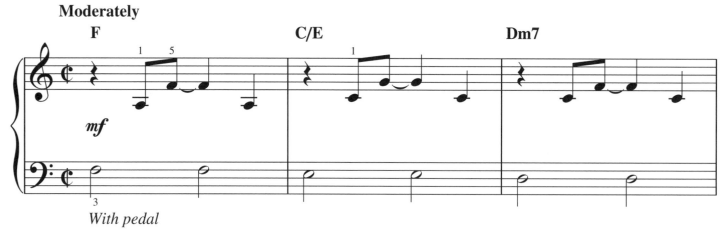

With pedal

I took my love and I took it down.

I climbed a

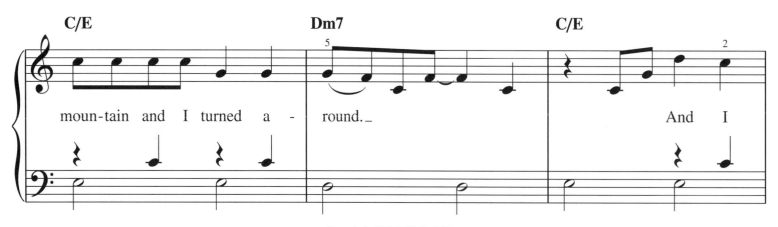

moun-tain and I turned a - round. And I

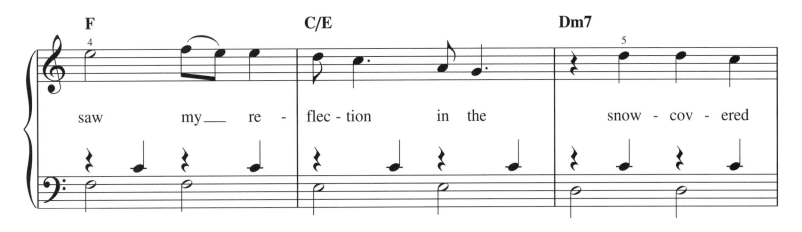

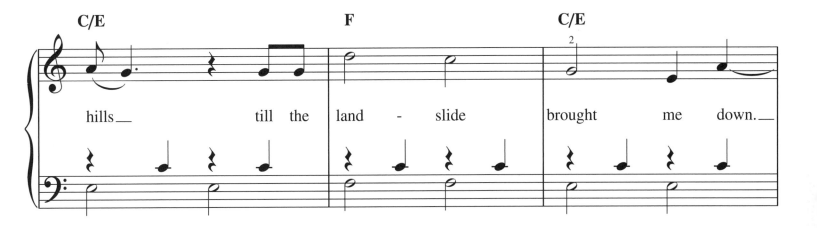

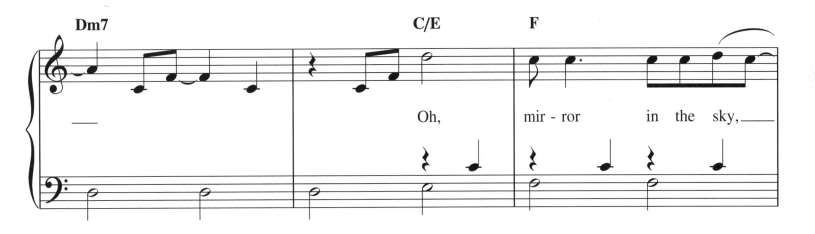

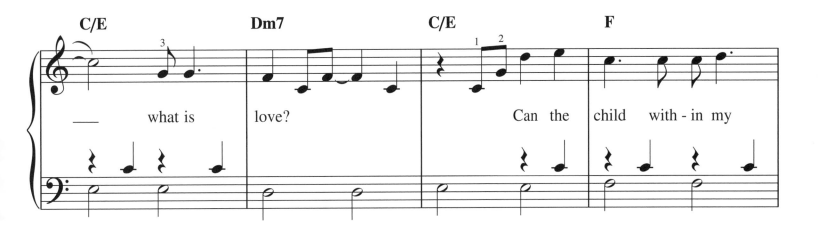

heart rise a - bove?   Can I

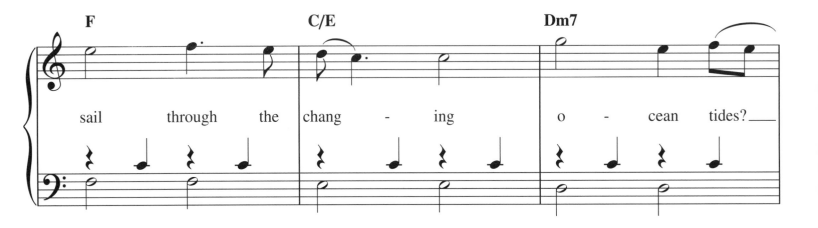

sail through the chang - ing o - cean tides?

 Can I han - dle the sea - sons of

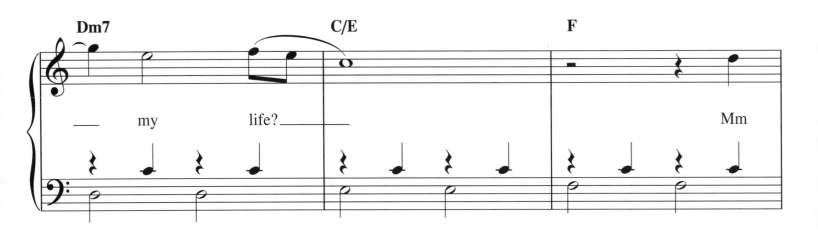

 my life?   Mm

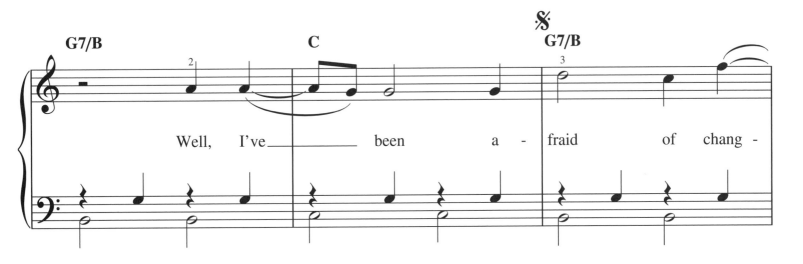

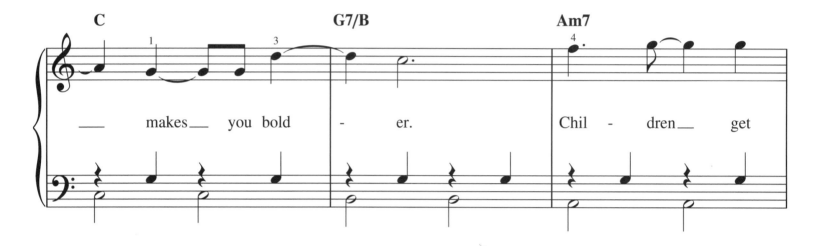

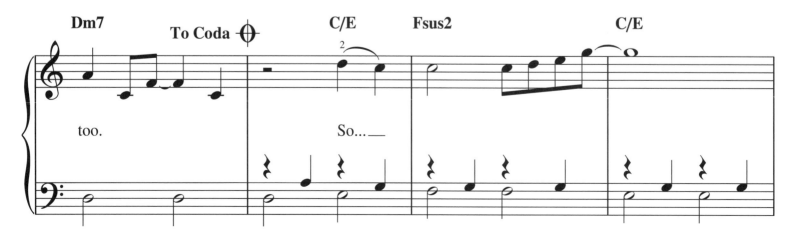

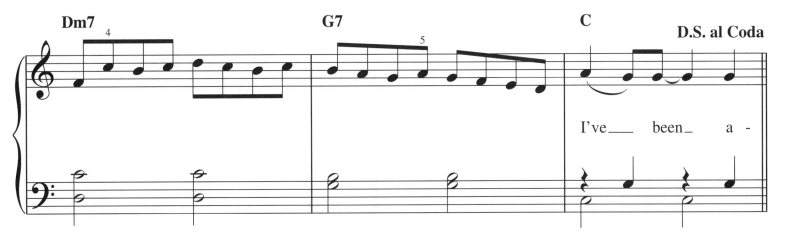

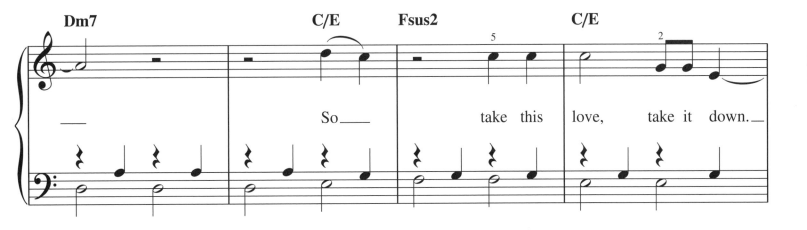

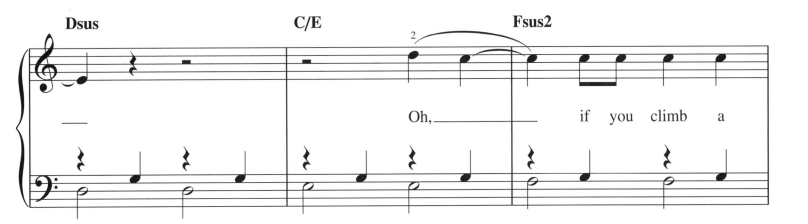

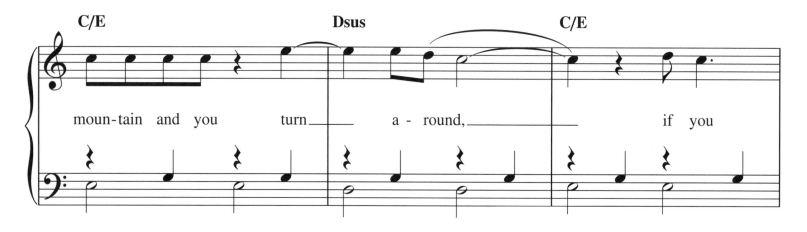

moun-tain and you turn ___ a - round, ___ if you

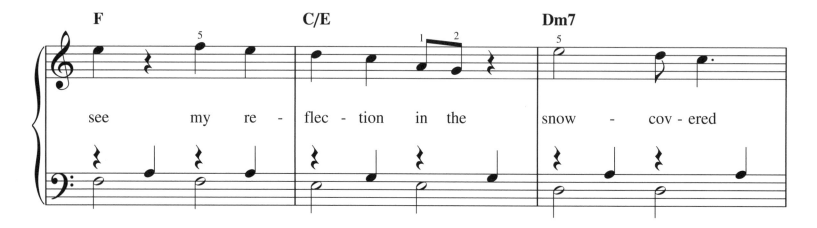

see my re - flec - tion in the snow - cov - ered

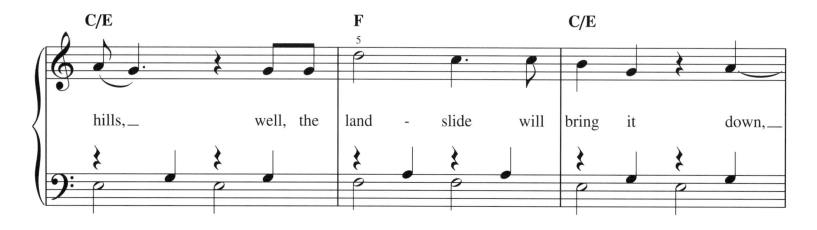

hills, ___ well, the land - slide will bring it down, ___

___ down. ___ And if you see my re - flec -

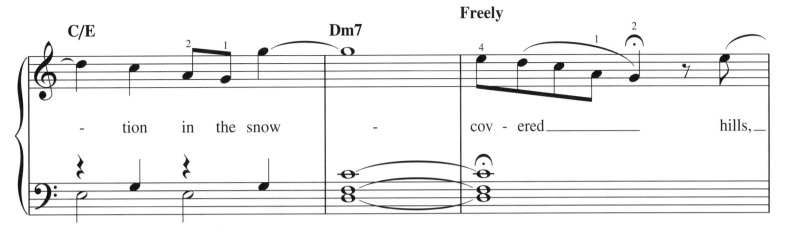

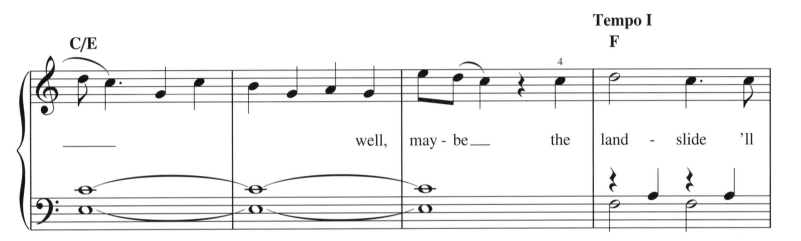

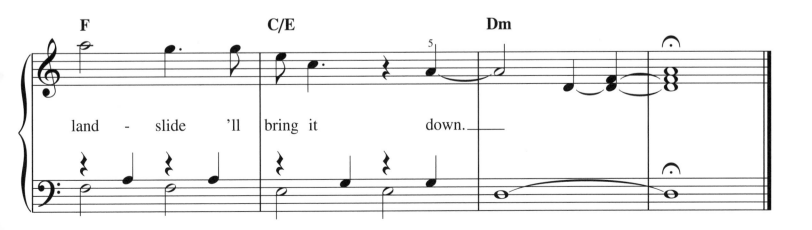

LEAVING ON A JET PLANE

Words and Music by
JOHN DENVER

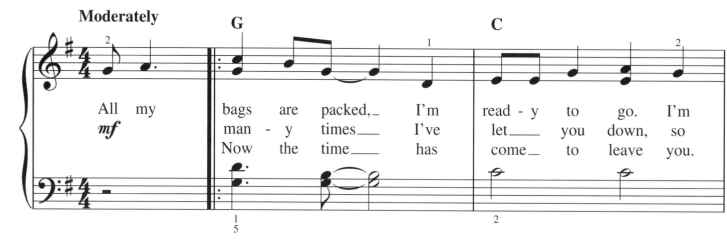

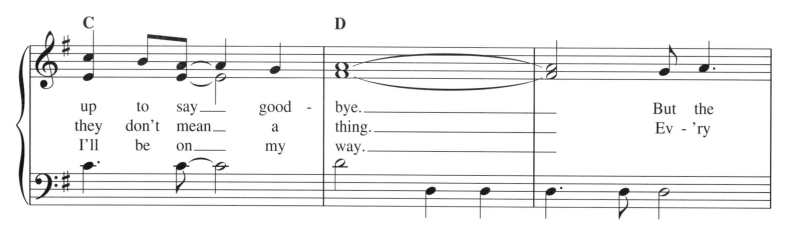

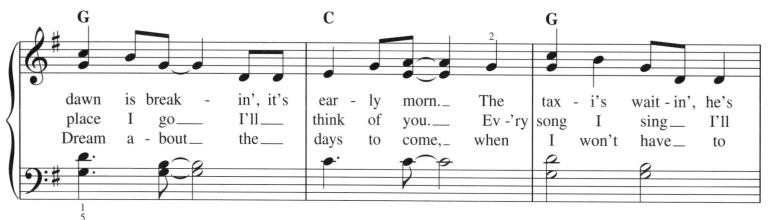

blow - in' his horn.___ Al - read - y I'm so
sing for you.___ When I come back I'll
leave a - lone,___ a - bout the times___

lone - some I could
bring your wed - ding
I won't have to

die.___
ring.___
say:___

So kiss me and smile for me.___
So kiss me and smile for me.___
Kiss me and smile for me.___

Tell me that___ you'll wait for me.___ Hold me like___ you'll nev-er let me

go. 'Cause I'm leav - in' on a jet___ plane.

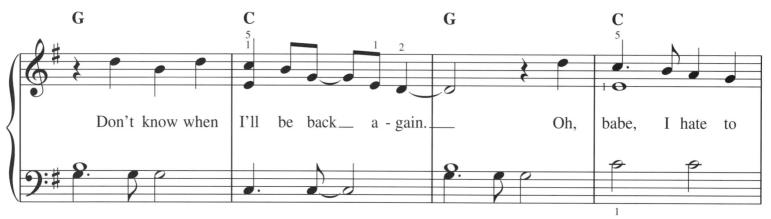

Don't know when I'll be back__ a-gain.__ Oh, babe, I hate to

1., 2.
go.__ (2.) There's so

3.
go.__ 'Cause I'm

leav - in' on a jet__ plane. Don't know when I'll be back__ a-gain.

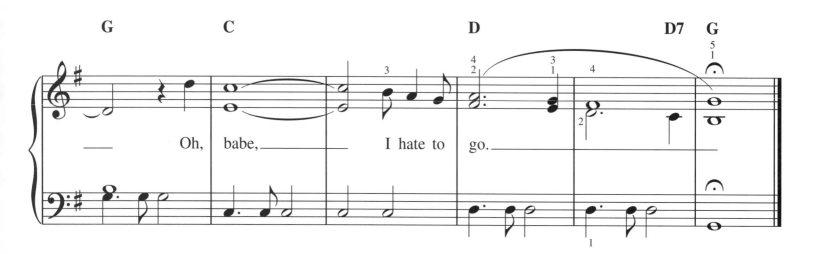

__ Oh, babe,__ I hate to go.__

NIGHT MOVES

Words and Music by
BOB SEGER

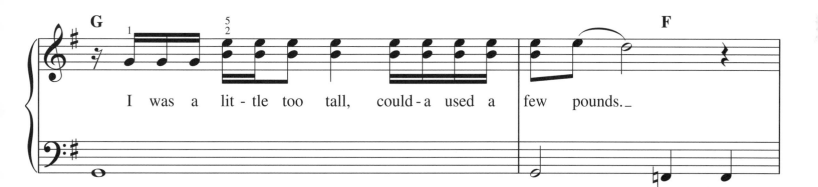

I was a lit-tle too tall, could-a used a few pounds.

Tight pants, points, hard-ly re-nown.

She was a black-haired beau-ty with big, dark eyes,_____

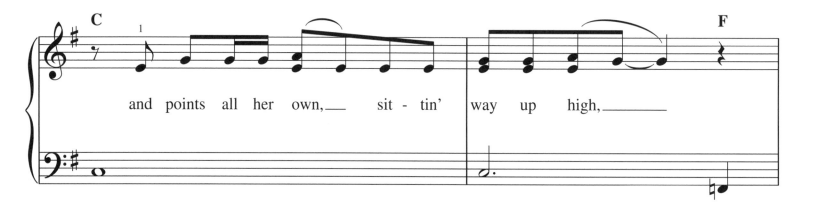

and points all her own,__ sit-tin' way up high,_____

way up firm and

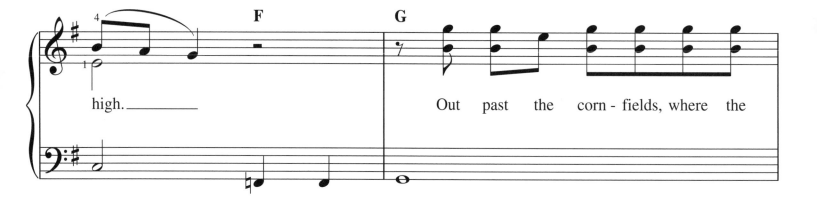

high._____ Out past the corn-fields, where the

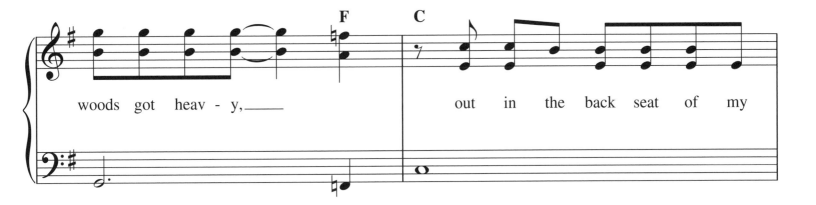

woods got heav - y,_____ out in the back seat of my

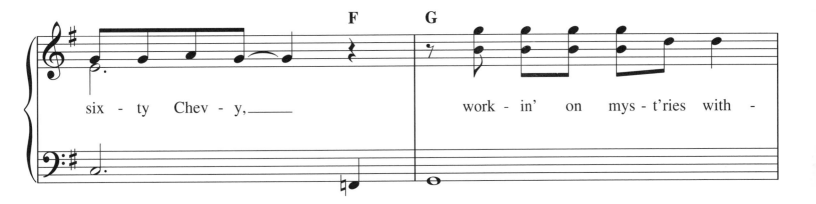

six - ty Chev - y,_____ work - in' on mys - t'ries with -

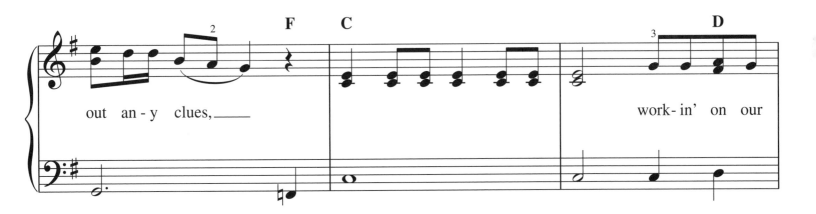

out an - y clues,_____ work - in' on our

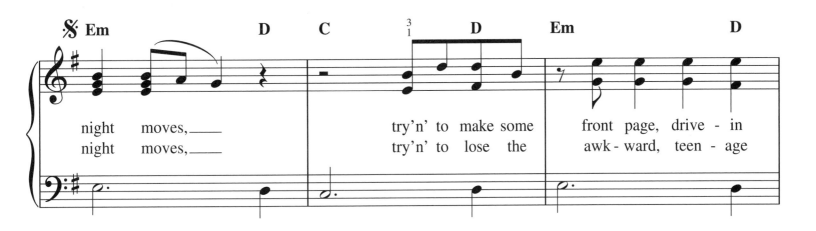

night moves,_____   try'n' to make some   front page, drive - in
night moves,_____   try'n' to lose the   awk - ward, teen - age

news. Work - in' on our night moves
blues, work - in' on our night moves.

in the sum - mer - time.
It was sum - mer - time.

Mm,
Mm,

in the sweet____ sum - mer - time.
sweet____ sum - mer - time.

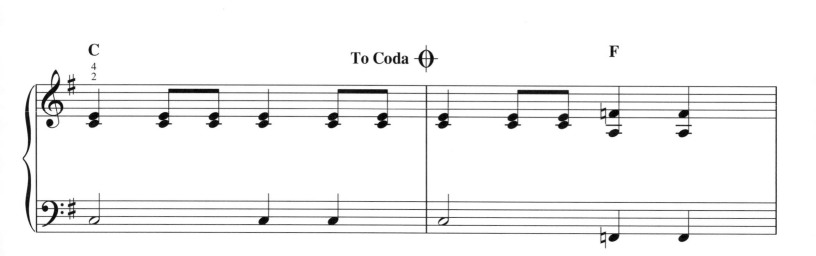

To Coda

We were-n't in love. Oh, no, far from it.

We were-n't search-in' for some pie - in - the - sky sum - mit.

We were just young and rest - less and bored,

liv - ing by the sword.

And we'd steal a - way ev - 'ry chance we could,

to the back room, to the al - ley, or the trust - y woods.

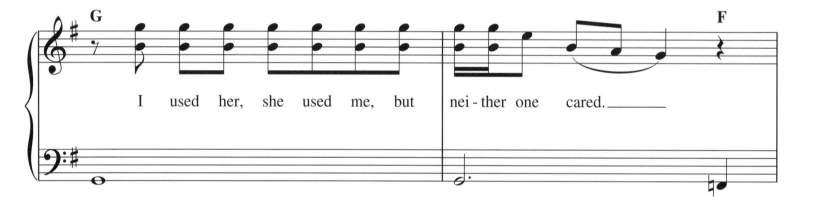

I used her, she used me, but nei - ther one cared.

D.S. al Coda

We were get - tin' our share, work - in' on our

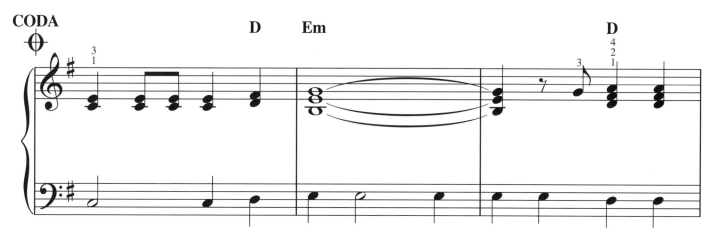

And, oh,_____   the

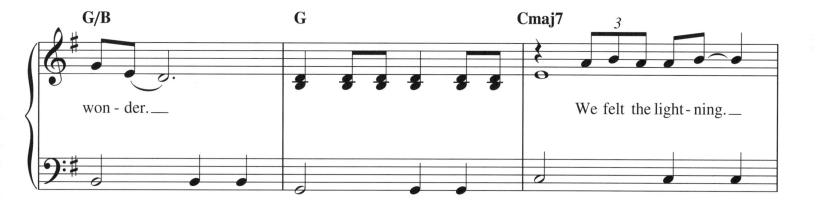

won - der.___   We felt the light - ning.___

Yeah,_____   and we wait - ed on the thun -

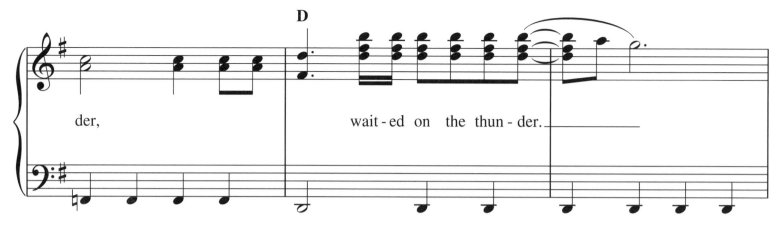

der,   wait-ed on the thun - der.____

Freely

I   a - woke last night   to the   sound   of   thun - der.____

Cmaj7

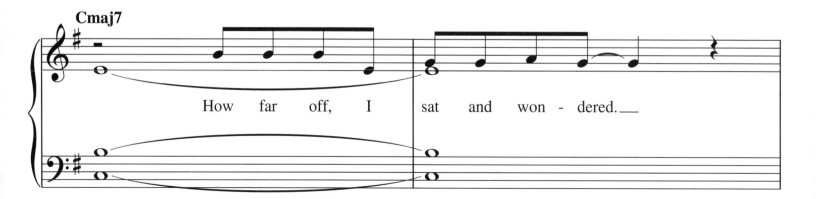

How   far   off,   I   sat   and   won - dered.____

81

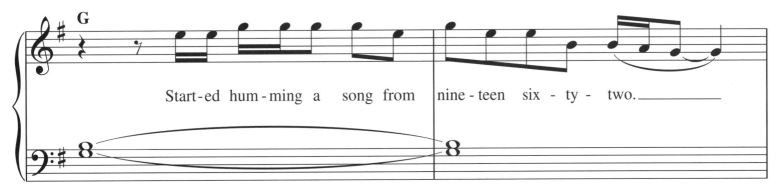

Start-ed hum-ming a song from nine-teen six-ty-two. _____

Ain't it fun-ny how the night moves? _____

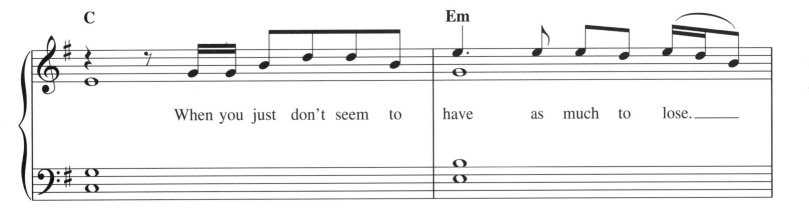

When you just don't seem to have as much to lose. _____

Strange how the night moves, _____ with au-tumn clos-ing

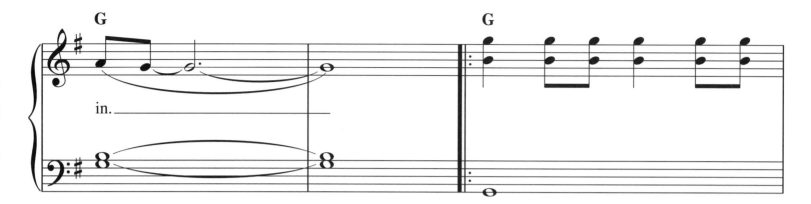

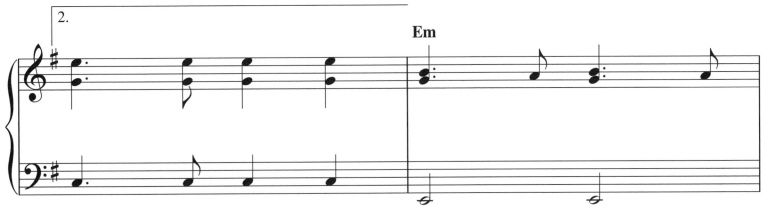

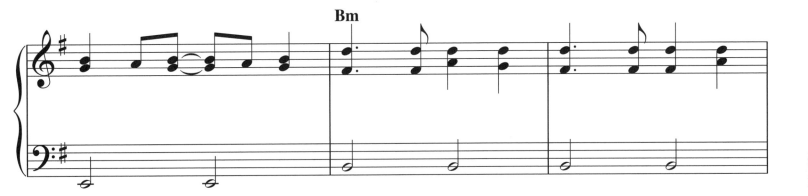

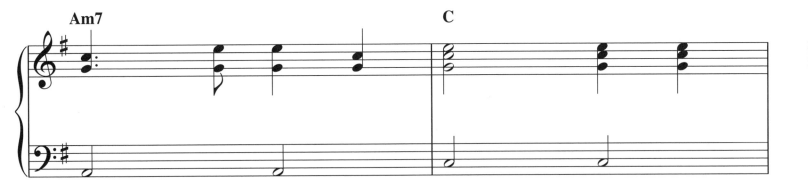

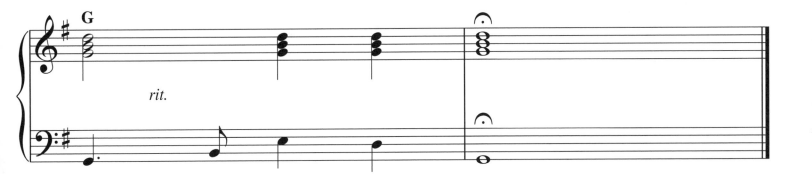

LONGER

Words and Music by
DAN FOGELBERG

Moderately slow

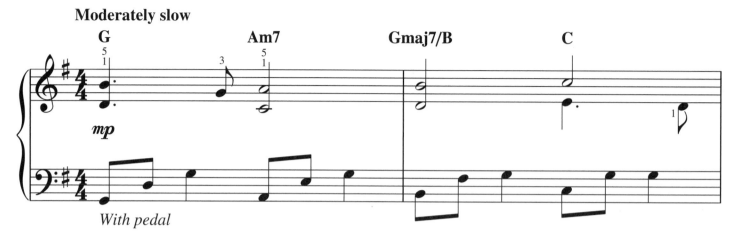

With pedal

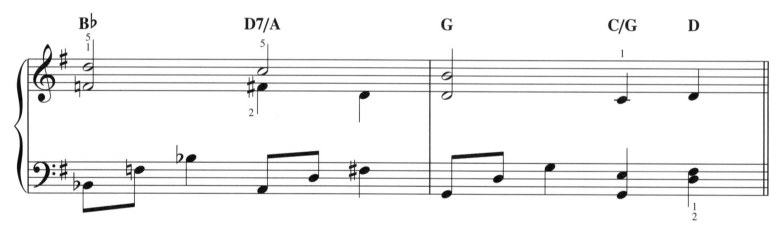

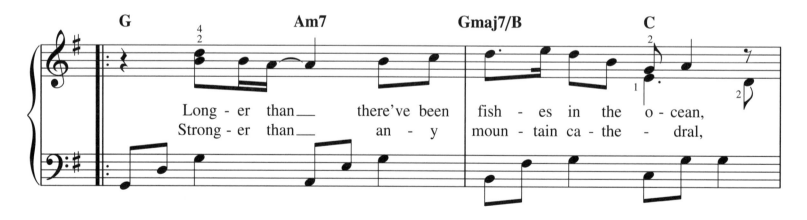

Long - er than___ there've been   fish - es in the o - cean,
Strong - er than___ an - y   moun - tain ca - the - dral,

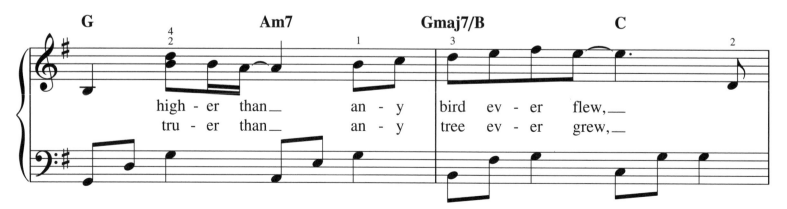

high - er than___ an - y   bird ev - er flew,___
tru - er than___ an - y   tree ev - er grew,___

long - er than___ there've been stars up in the heav - ens,
deep - er than___ an - y for - est pri - me - val,

I've been in love___ with you.
I am in love___ with you.

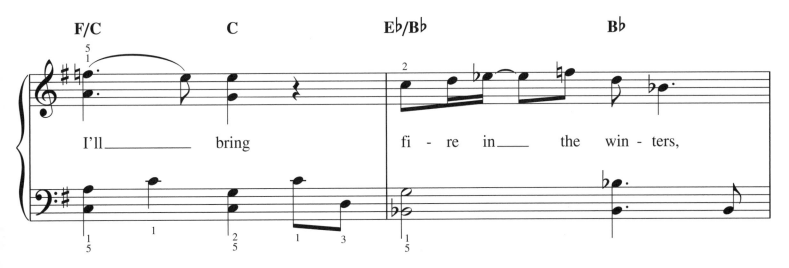

I'll_____ bring fi - re in___ the win - ters,

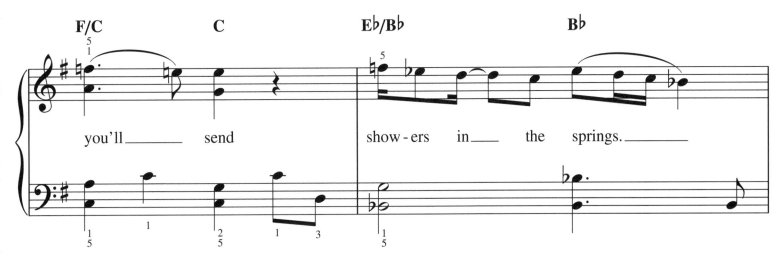

you'll_____ send show - ers in___ the springs.___

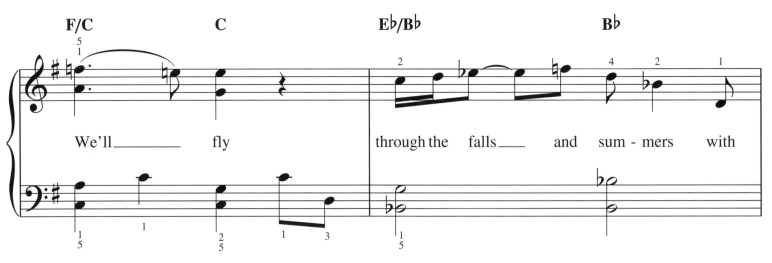

We'll_____ fly | through the falls____ and sum - mers with

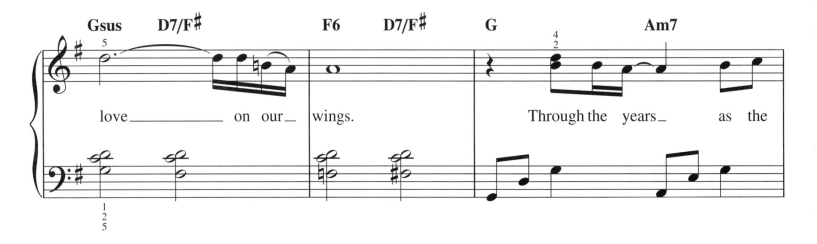

love_____ on our_ wings. | Through the years_ as the

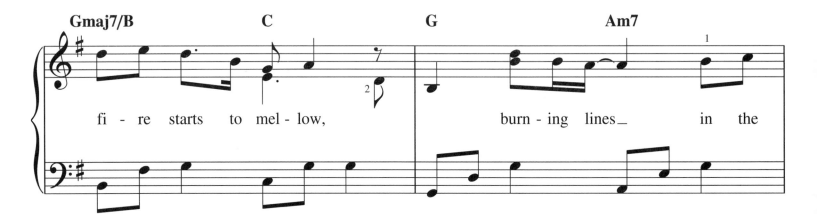

fi - re starts to mel - low, | burn - ing lines_ in the

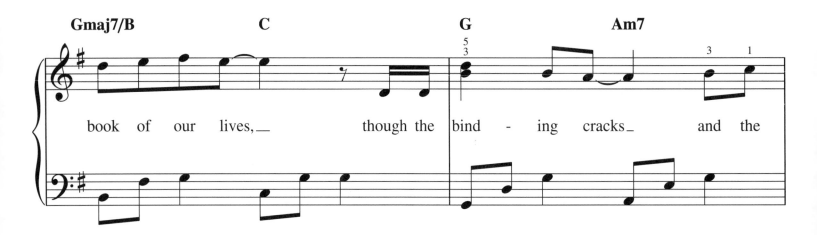

book of our lives,___ though the bind - ing cracks_ and the

pag - es start to yel - low, I'll be in love___ with you.___

I'll be in love___ with you.___

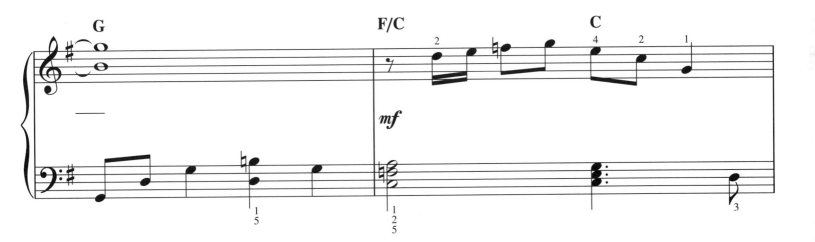

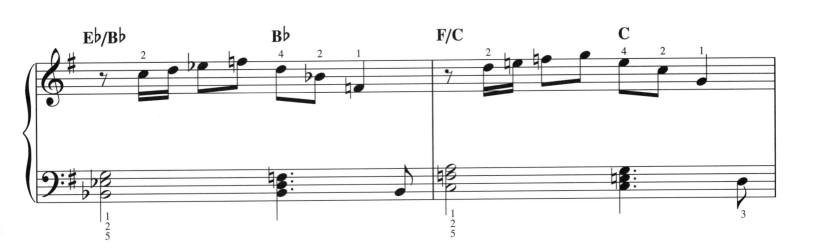

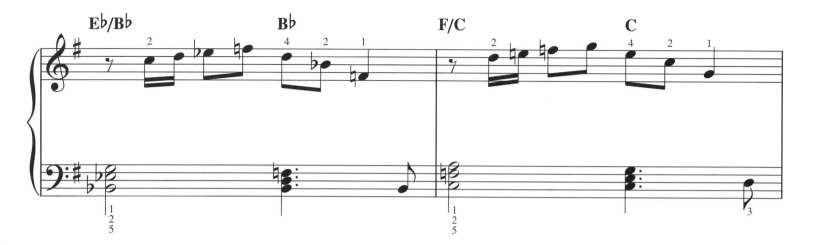

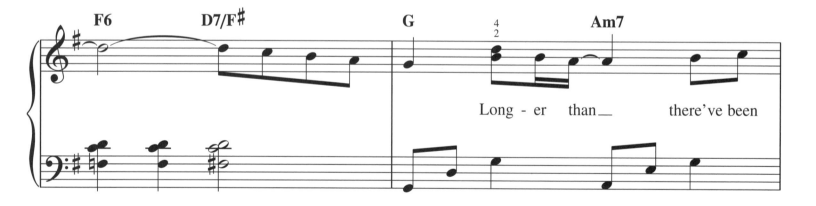

Long - er than__ there've been

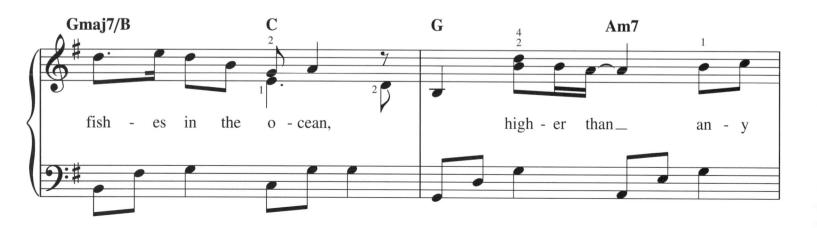

fish - es in the o - cean,

high - er than__ an - y

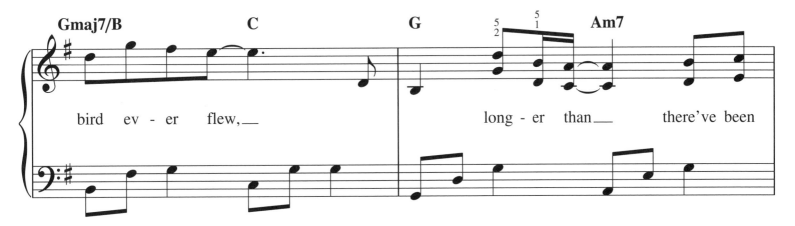

bird ev - er flew, ___ long - er than ___ there've been

stars up in the heav - ens, I've been in love ___ with you. ___

I am in love ___ with you. ___

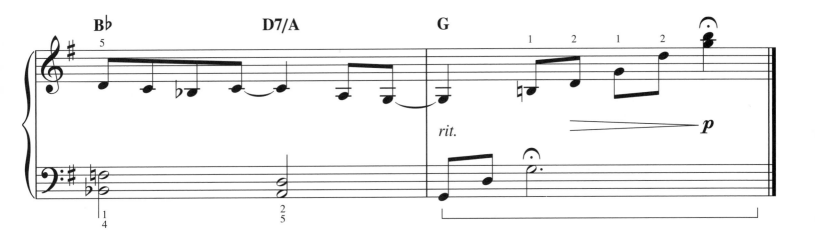

rit. _____ p

MORE THAN WORDS

Words and Music by NUNO BETTENCOURT
and GARY CHERONE

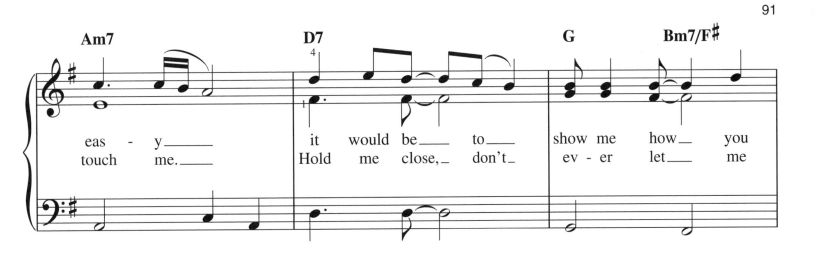

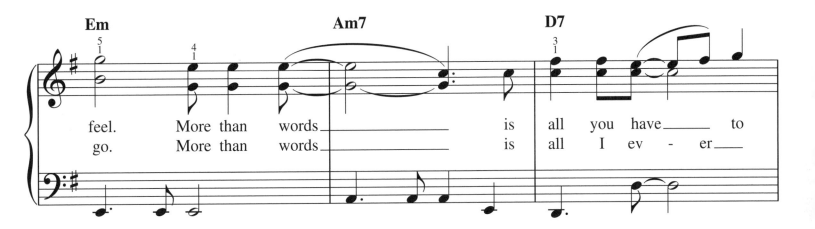

read - y_____ know.	What

would	you	do____

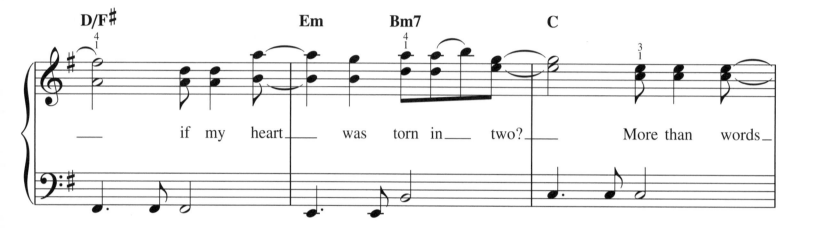

____	if my heart____	was torn in___ two?____	More than	words_

____	to show_ you feel____	that your	love____	for	me___	is____

real.	What	would	you	say____	if I	took_

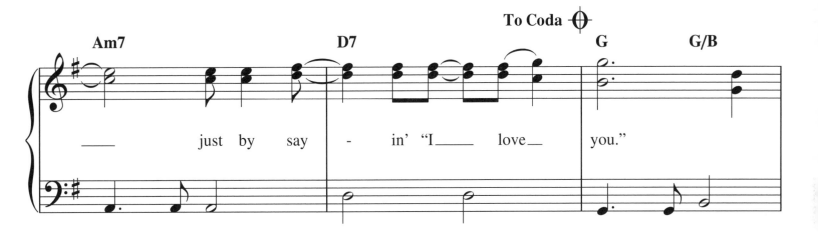

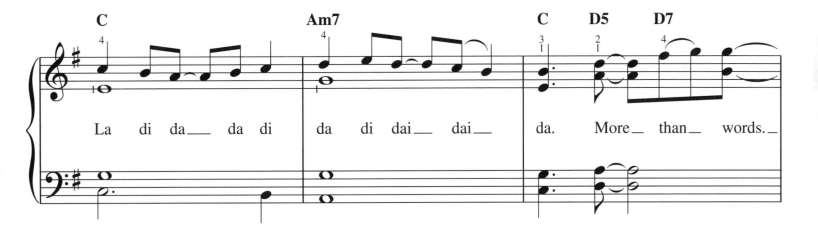

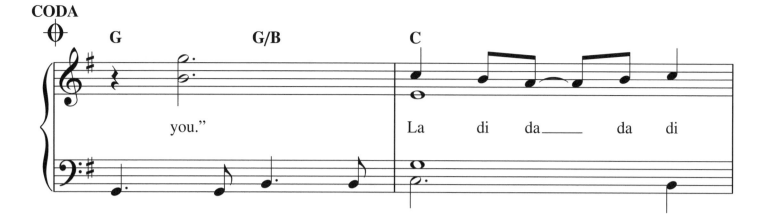

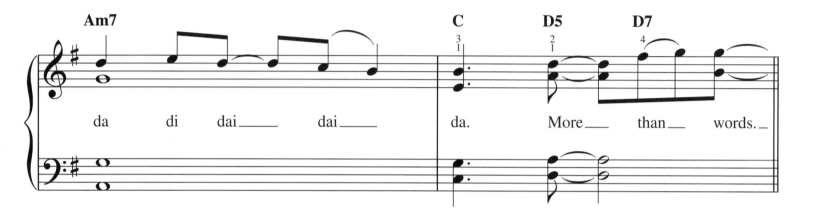

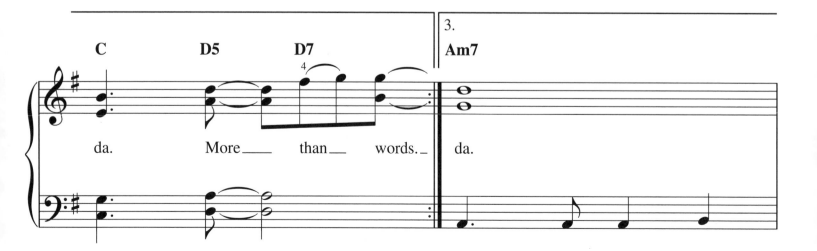

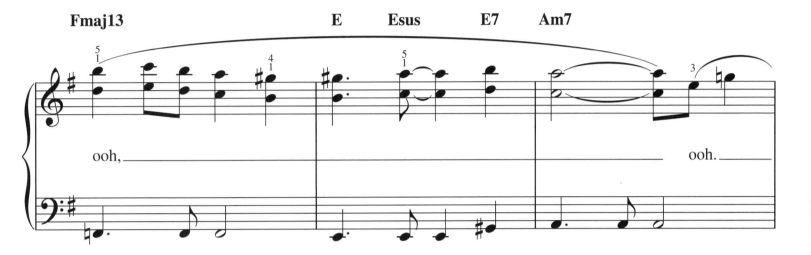

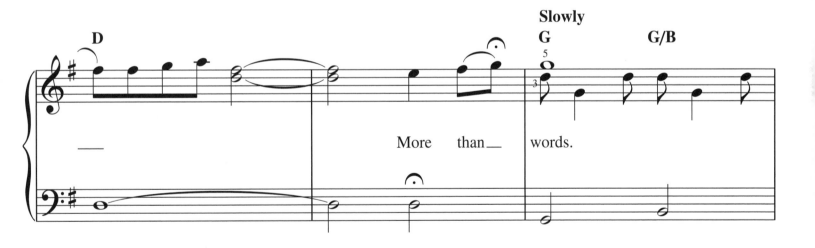

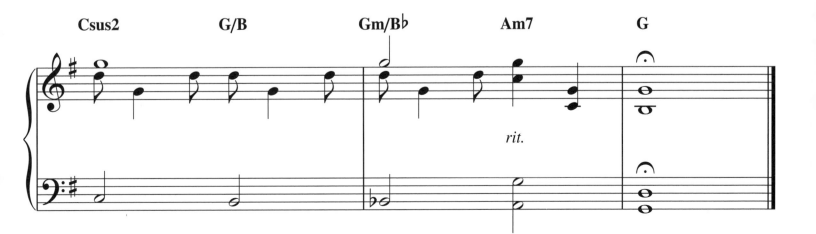

NORWEGIAN WOOD
(This Bird Has Flown)

Words and Music by JOHN LENNON
and PAUL McCARTNEY

Moderately flowing, in 1

I *mp* once had a girl, or should I

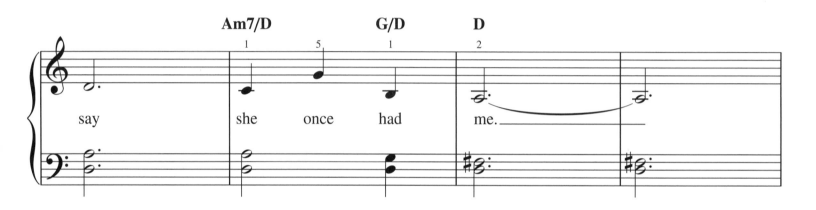

say she once had me. ____

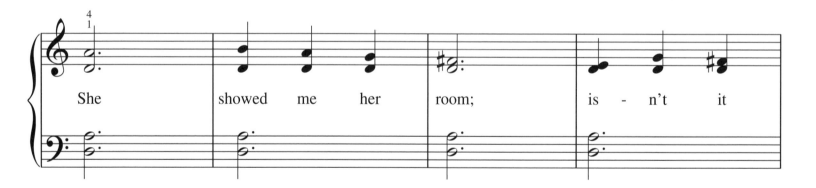

She showed me her room; is - n't it

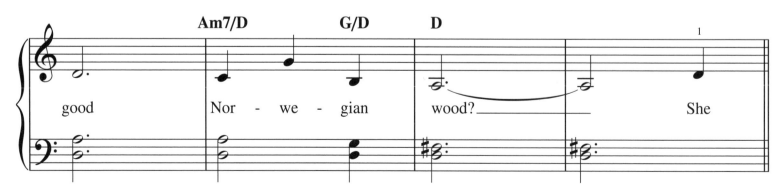

good Nor - we - gian wood? ____ She

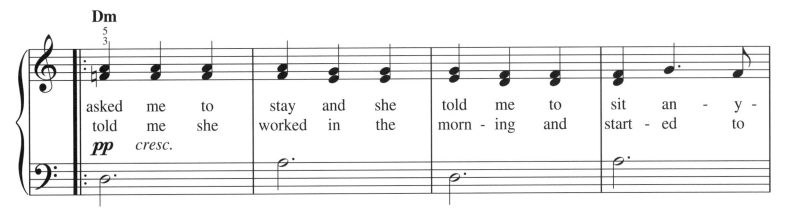

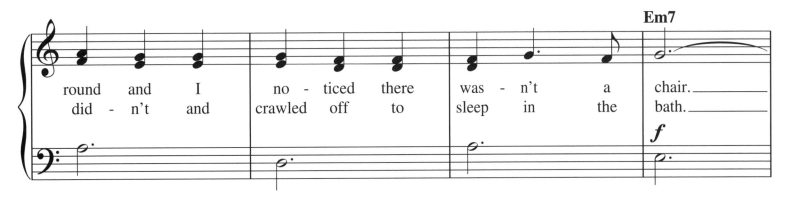

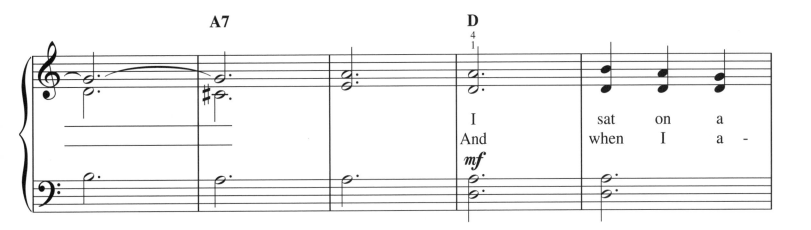

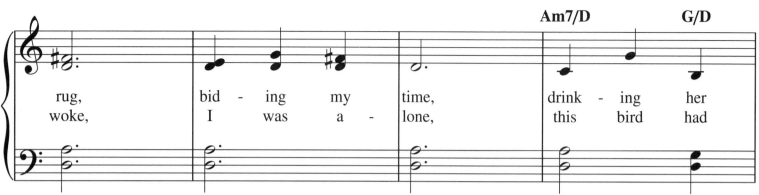

rug, bid - ing my time, drink - ing her
woke, I was a - lone, this bird her had

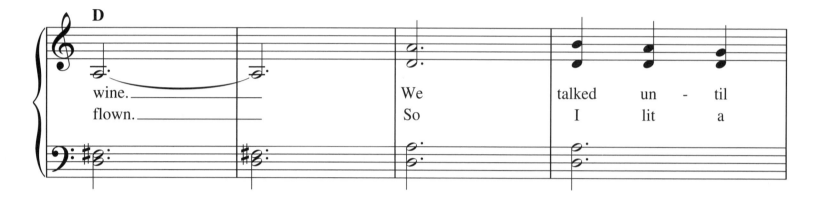

wine. We talked un - til
flown. So I lit a

two, and then she said, "It's time for
fire; is - n't it good Nor - we - gian

2nd time, much slower

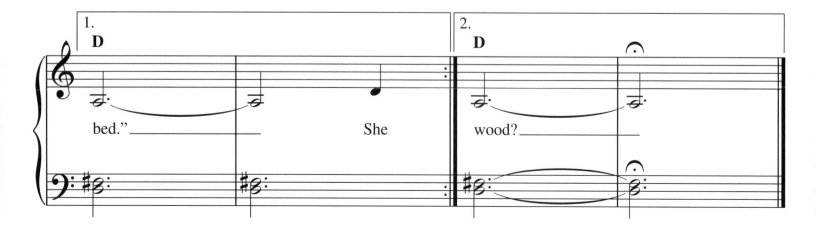

1.
bed." She

2.
wood?

SEVEN BRIDGES ROAD

Words and Music by
STEPHEN T. YOUNG

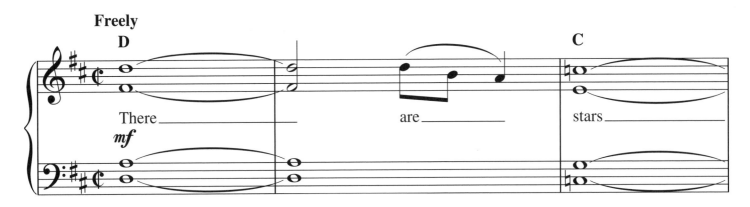

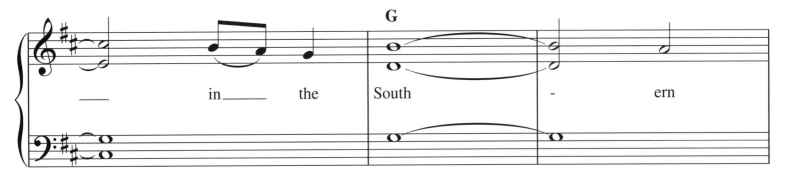

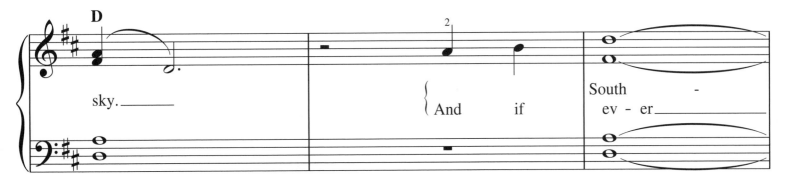

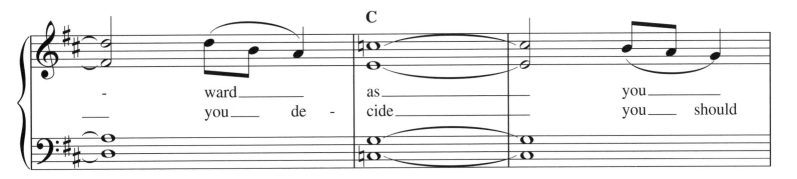

100

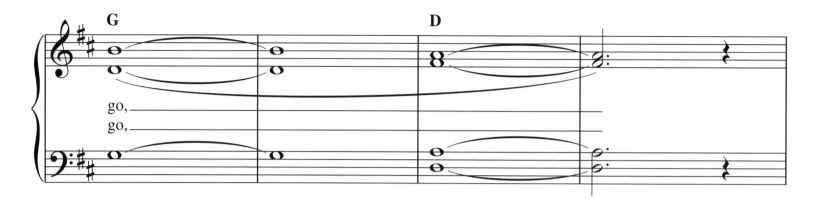

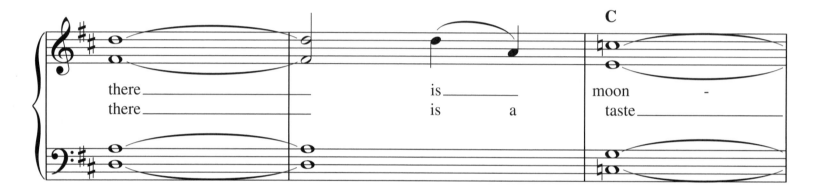

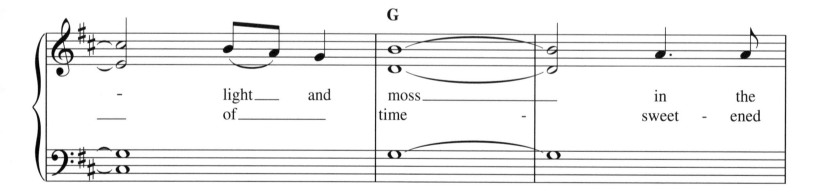

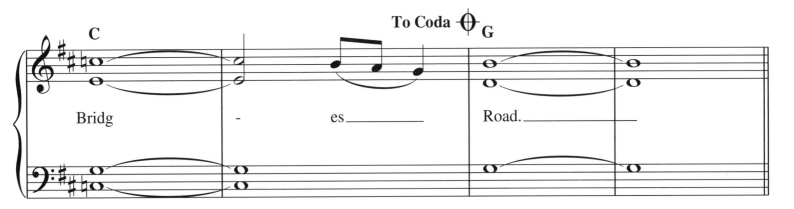

Bridg - es _____ Road. _____

Bright Country

Now,

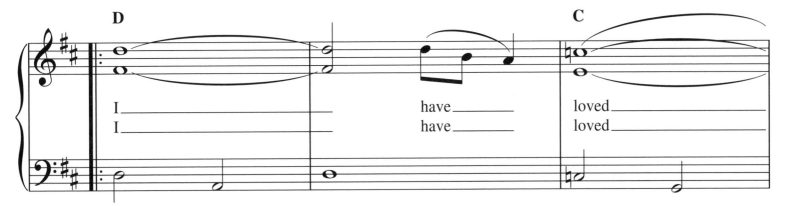

I _____ have _____ loved _____
I _____ have _____ loved _____

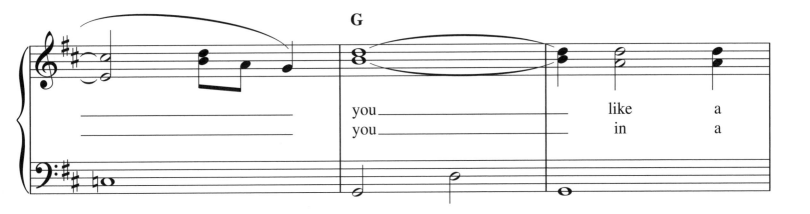

you _____ like a
you _____ in a

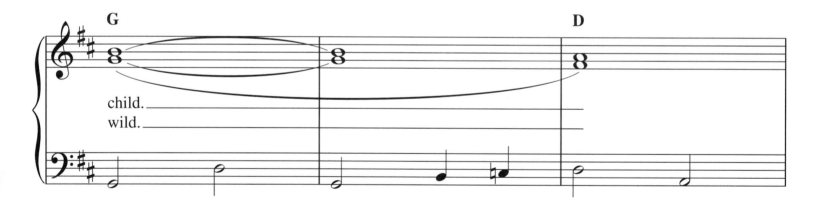

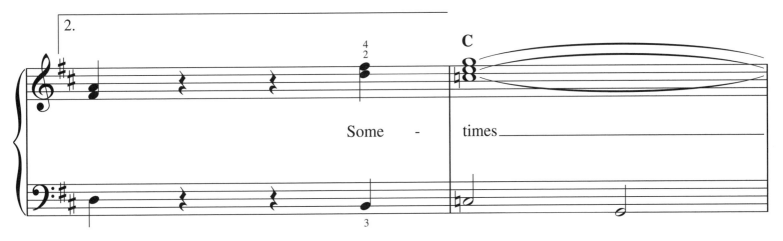

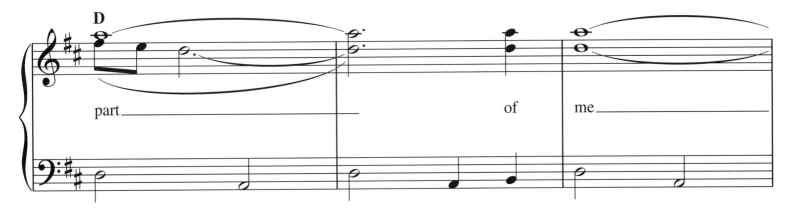

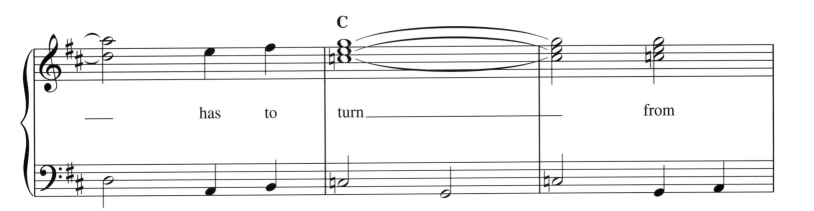

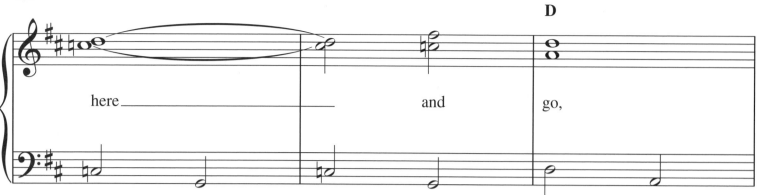

here _____ and go,

run - ning like a child _____

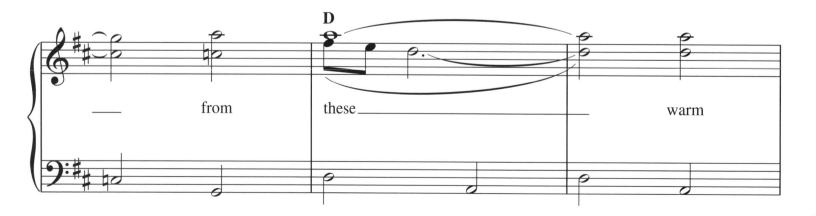

___ from these _____ warm

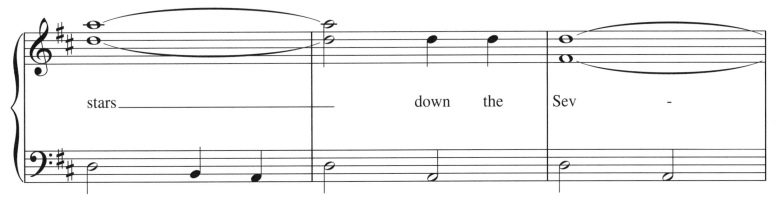

stars _____ down the Sev -

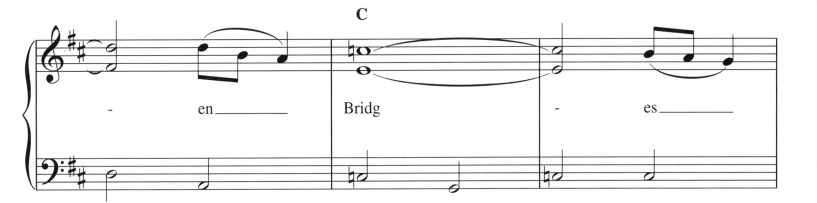

- en _____ Bridg - es _____

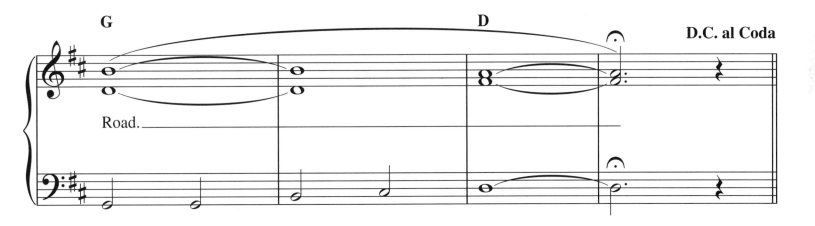

D.C. al Coda

Road. _____

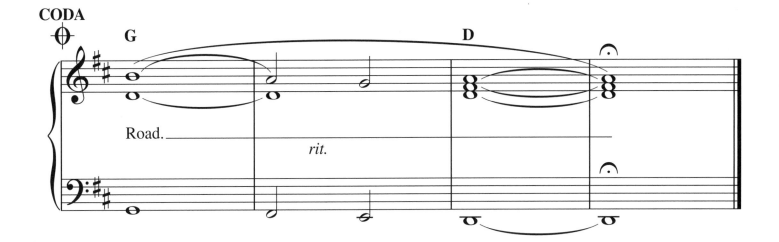

CODA

Road. _____

rit.

SUITE: JUDY BLUE EYES

Words and Music by
STEPHEN STILLS

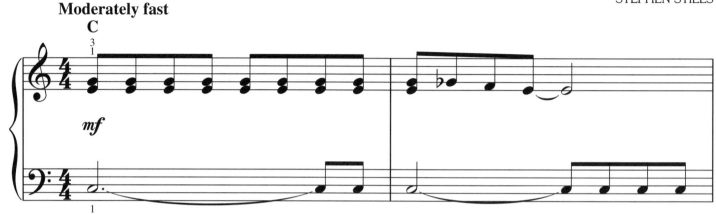

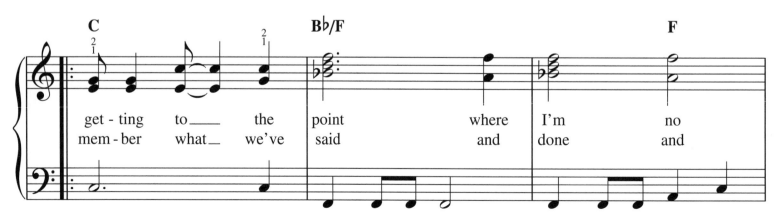

get-ting to____ the point where I'm no and
mem-ber what__ we've said and done

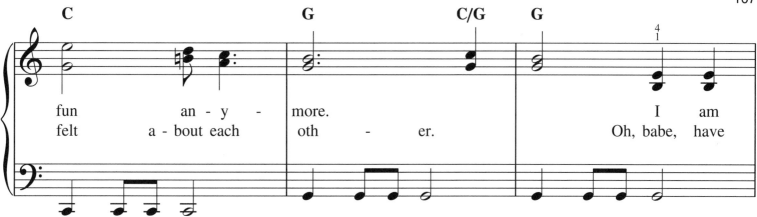

fun an - y - more.
felt a - bout each oth - er.
I am
Oh, babe, have

sor - ry.
mer - cy.
Some - times it
Don't let the

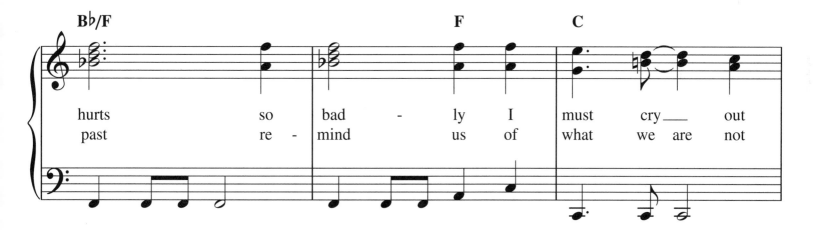

hurts so bad - ly I
past re - mind us of
must cry___ out
what we are not

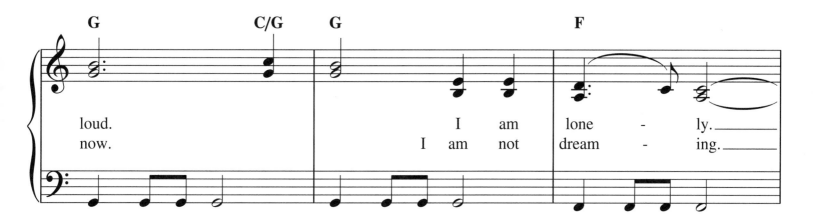

loud.
now.
I am
I am not
lone - ly.___
dream - ing.___

I am   yours,   you are   mine,   you are

what you   are.   You make   it____   hard._____

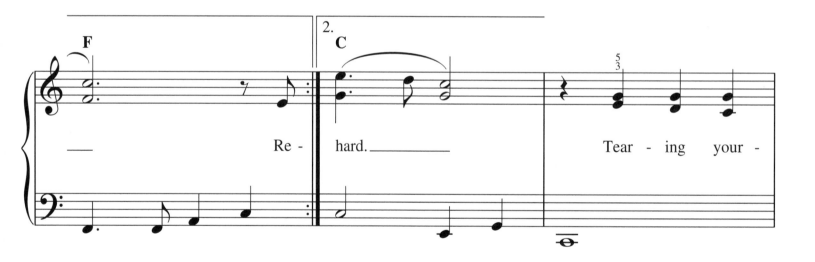

____   a - way   Re -   hard._____   Tear - ing   your -

self____   a - way   from__ me   now,_____ you are

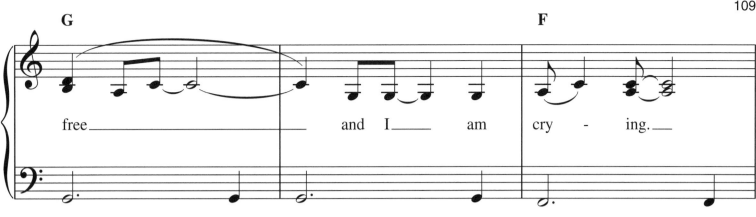

free_____ and I____ am cry - ing.__

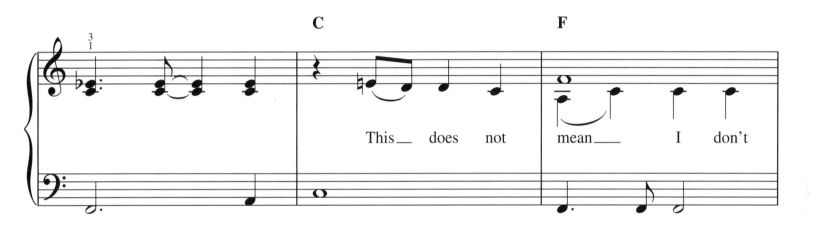

This__ does not mean____ I don't

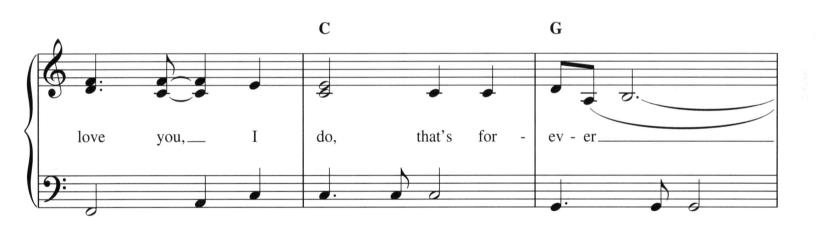

love you,___ I do, that's for - ev - er_____

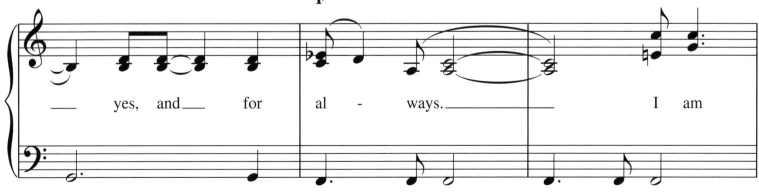

___ yes, and__ for al - ways._____ I am

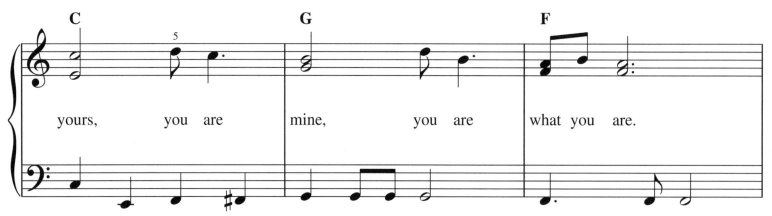

yours,   you are   mine,   you are   what you are.

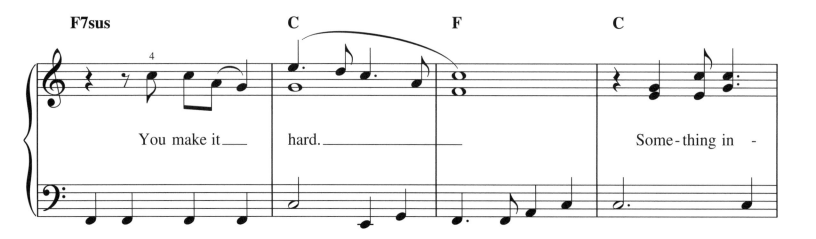

You make it____ hard._____   Some-thing in -

side   is   tell - ing me____ that   I've got____ your

se - cret.   Are you still   lis - t'ning?

F7sus   C   B♭/F

Fear is___ the lock and

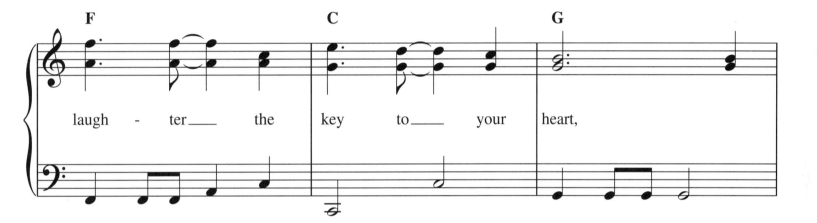

F   C   G

laugh - ter___ the key to___ your heart,

F

and I love_____ you._____ I am

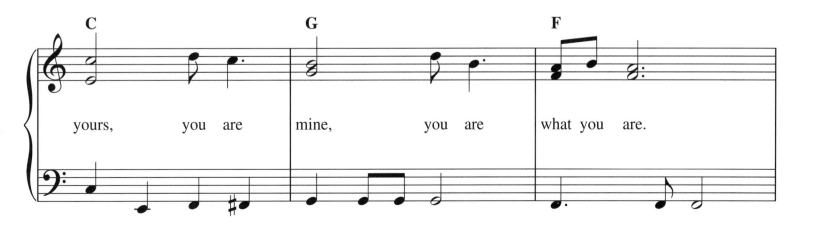

C   G   F

yours, you are mine, you are what you are.

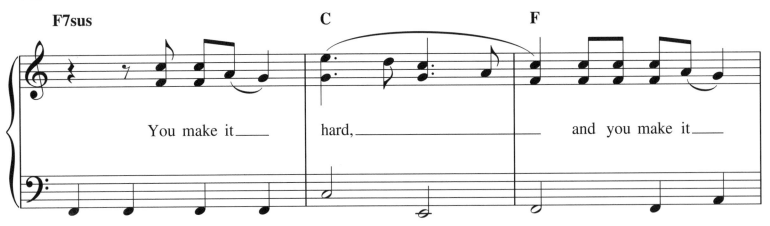

You make it____ hard,_____ and you make it____

hard,_____ and you make it____ hard,_____

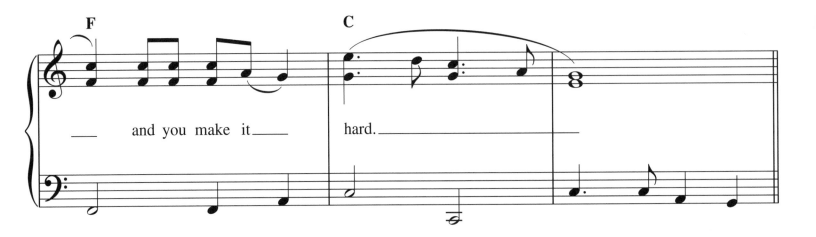

____ and you make it____ hard._____

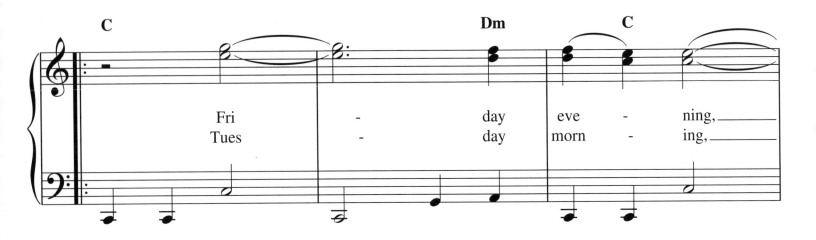

Fri - day eve - ning,_____
Tues - day morn - ing,_____

Sun - day in the
please ____ be gone, I'm

af - ter - noon. ____
tired of you. ____

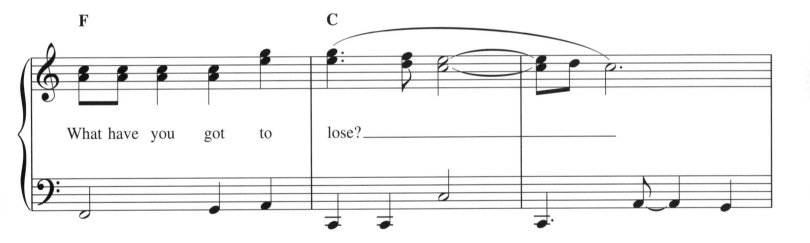

What have you got to lose? ____

1.

2.

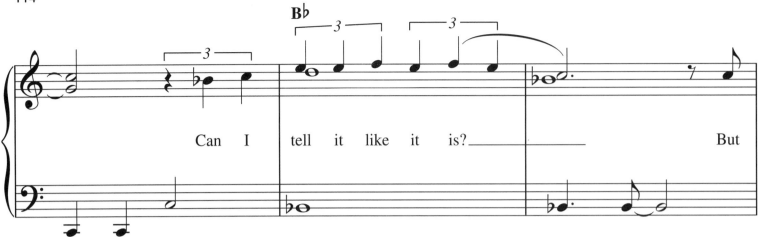

Can I tell it like it is?_____ But

lis - ten to me, ba - by._____ It's my heart__

_____ that's a - suf - f'rin'. It's a - dy - in'. And that's what I_____ have to

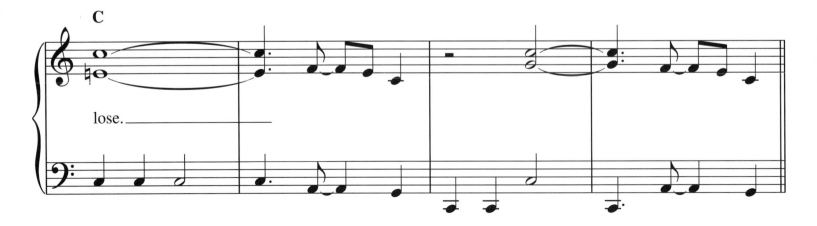

lose._____

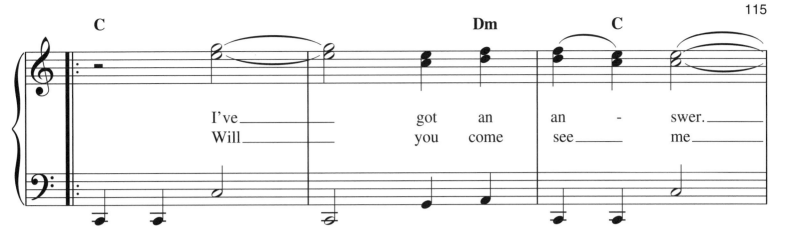

I've ____ got an an - swer.____
Will ____ you come see ____ me ____

____
____
I'm ____ go - ing ____ to
Thurs - days and

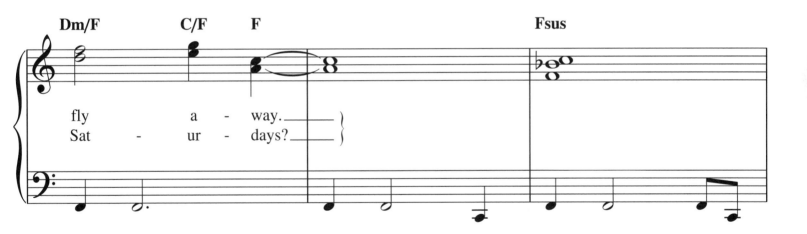

fly a - way.____
Sat - ur - days?____

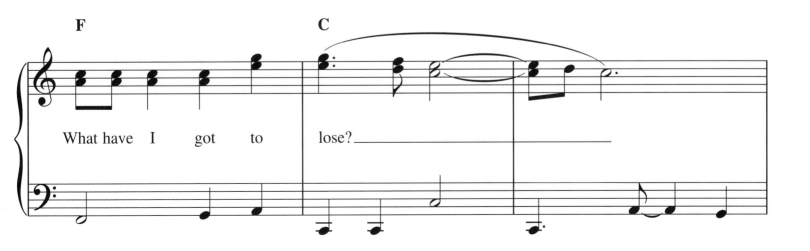

What have I got to lose?____

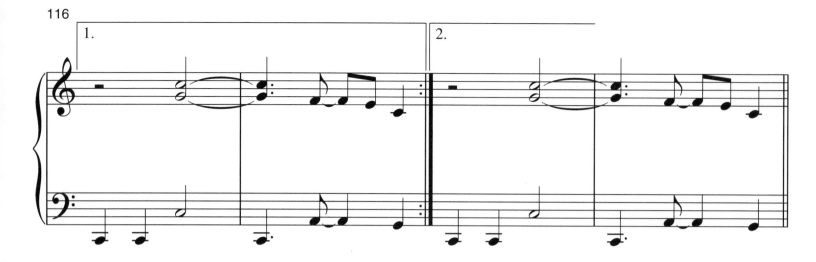

Bb/C ... **C**

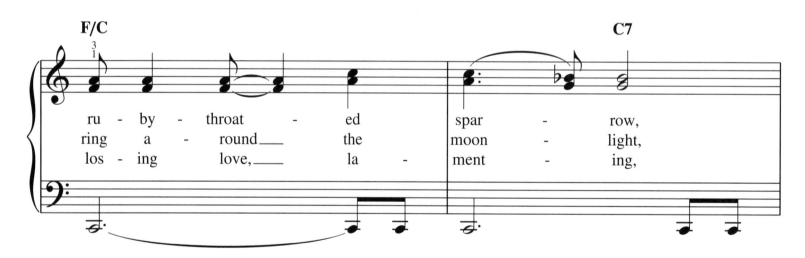

Chest - nut   brown___   ca - nar - y,_____
Voic - es   of___   the   an - gels,_____
Lac - y,   lilt - ing   lyr - ic,_____

F/C ... **C7**

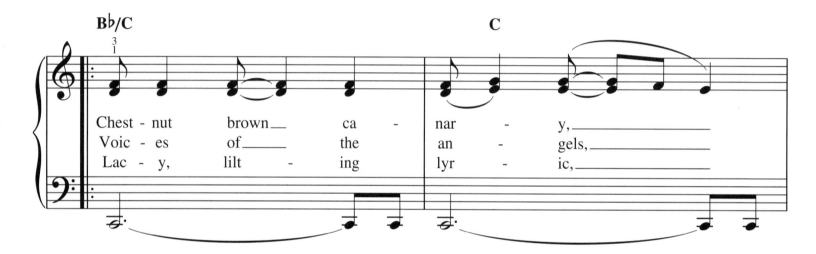

ru - by - throat - ed   spar - row,
ring a - round___ the   moon - light,
los - ing   love,___ la - ment - ing,

Bb/C

sing   a   song,___   don't   be   long,___
ask - ing   me, said   she   so   free,___
change   my   life,___   make   it   right,___

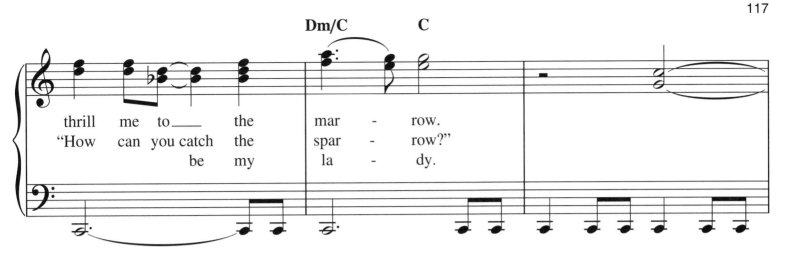

thrill me to____ the mar - row.
"How can you catch the spar - row?"
be my la - dy.

Play 3 times

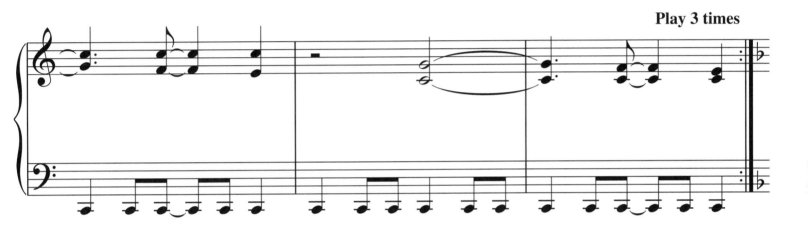

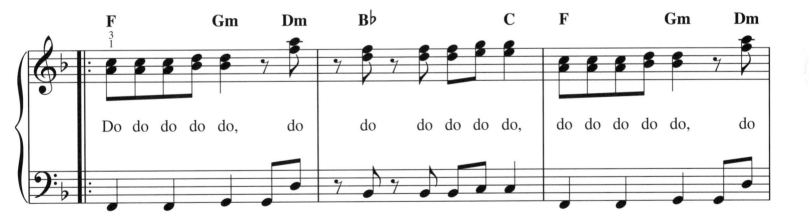

Do do do do do, do do do do do do, do do do do do, do

1., 2.

do do do.

3.

do do do.

TAKE ME HOME, COUNTRY ROADS

Words and Music by JOHN DENVER,
BILL DANOFF and TAFFY NIVERT

Moderately, in 2

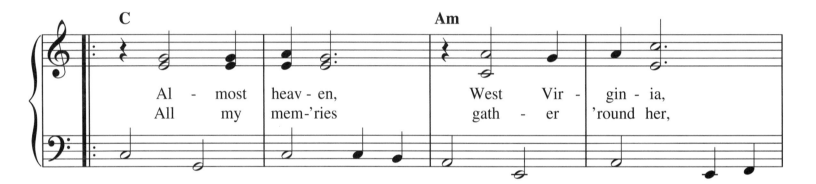

Al - most heav - en, West Vir - gin - ia,
All my mem-'ries gath - er 'round her,

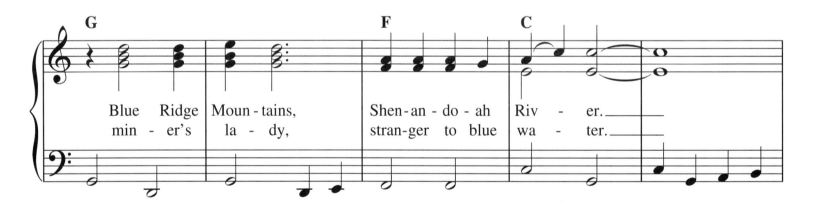

Blue Ridge Moun - tains, Shen-an-do-ah Riv - er.
min - er's la - dy, stran-ger to blue wa - ter.

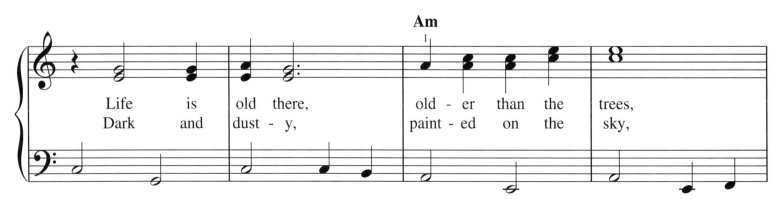

Life is old there, old - er than the trees,
Dark and dust - y, paint - ed on the sky,

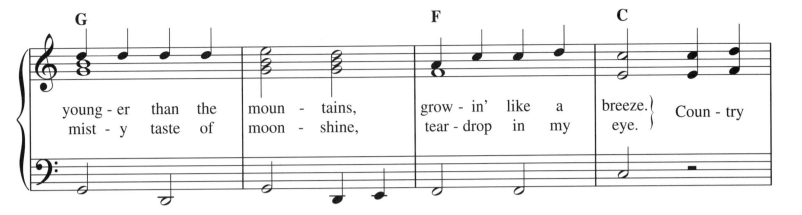

younger than the mountains, growin' like a breeze.
mist-y taste of moonshine, teardrop in my eye.
Country

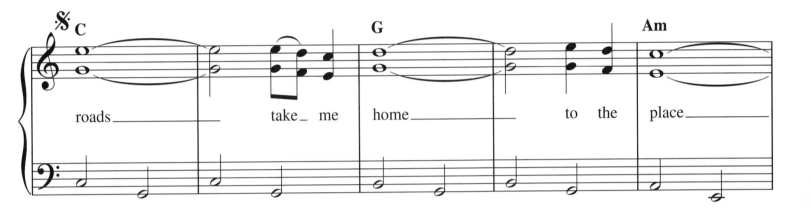

roads take me home to the place

I belong: West Virginia, mountain

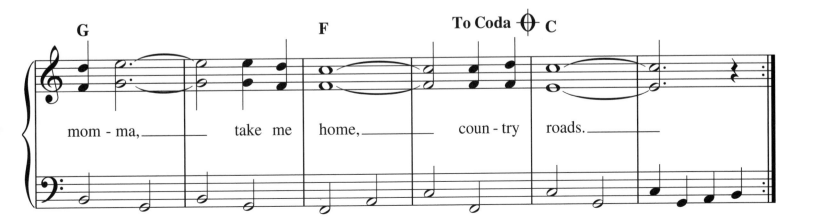

momma, take me home, country roads.

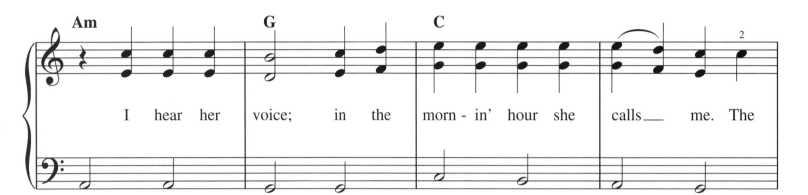

I hear her voice; in the morn - in' hour she calls___ me. The

ra - di - o re - minds me of my home far a - way. And

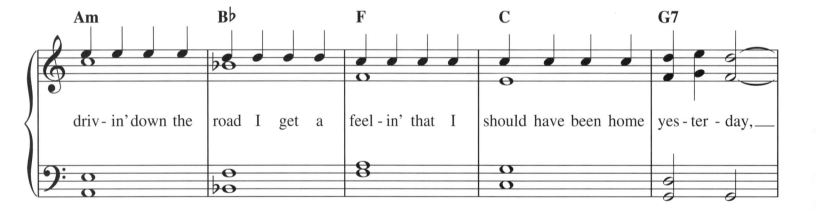

driv - in' down the road I get a feel - in' that I should have been home yes - ter - day,___

D.S. al Coda

___ yes - ter - day.___ Coun - try

CODA

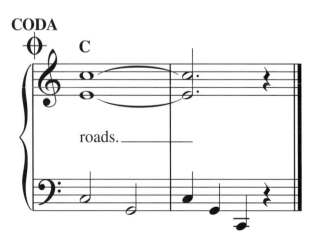

roads.___

TIME IN A BOTTLE

Words and Music by
JIM CROCE

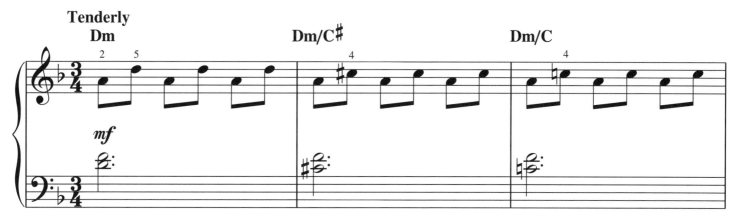

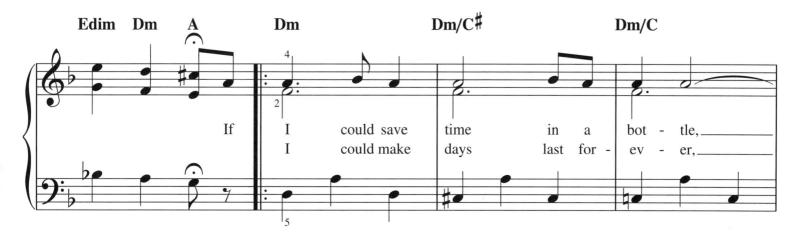

If I could save time in a bot - tle,
I could make days last for - ev - er,

the first thing that I'd like to do,
if words could make wish - es come true;

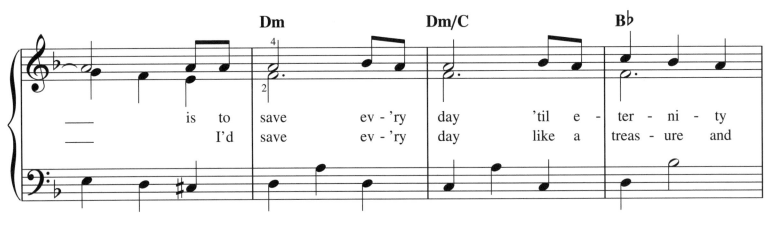

is to save ev - 'ry day 'til e - ter - ni - ty
I'd save ev - 'ry day like a treas - ure and

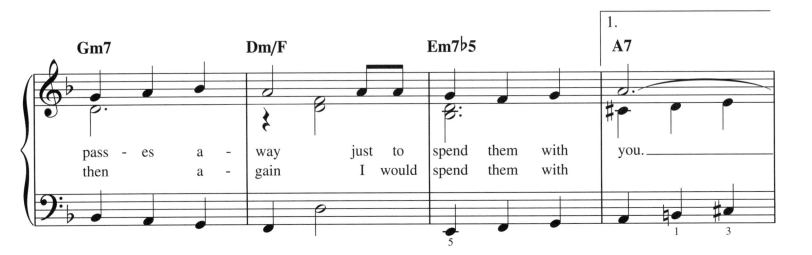

pass - es a - way just to spend them with you.
then a - gain I would spend them with

If you. But there nev - er seems to

be e - nough time to do the things you want to do once you

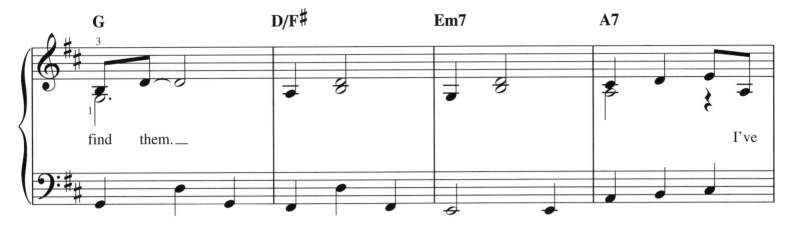

find them.___

looked a - round   e - nough to   know___ that   you're the one   I   want to   go   through

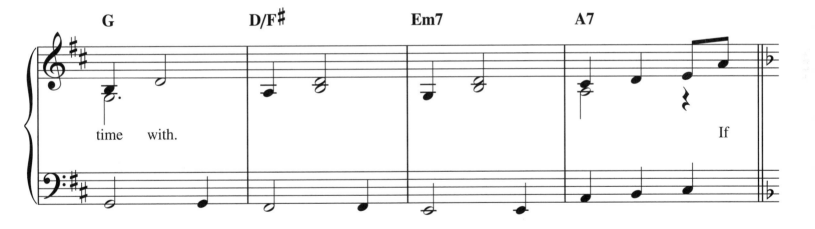

time   with.

If

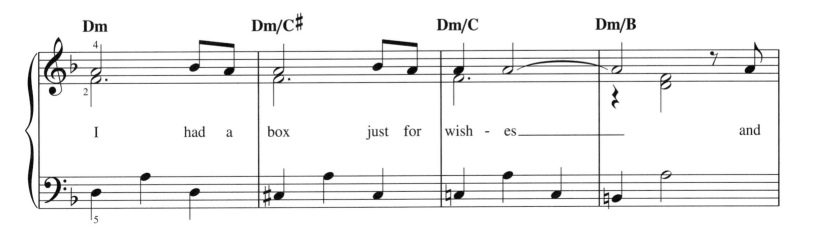

I   had a   box   just for   wish - es___   and

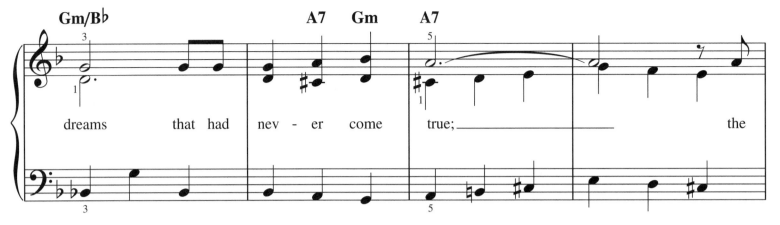

dreams   that had   nev - er   come   true;_____   the

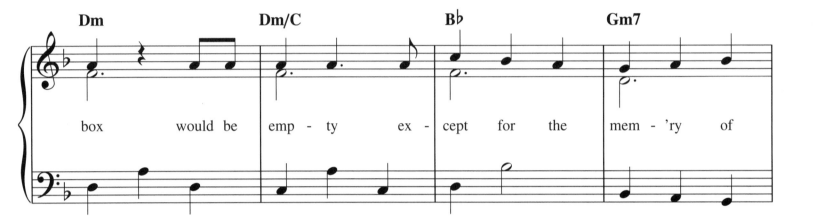

box   would be   emp - ty   ex -   cept   for   the   mem - 'ry   of

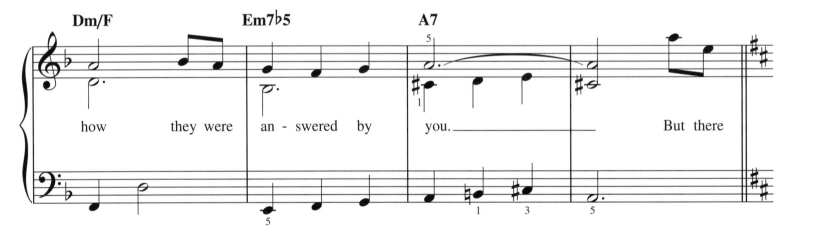

how   they were   an - swered   by   you._____   But there

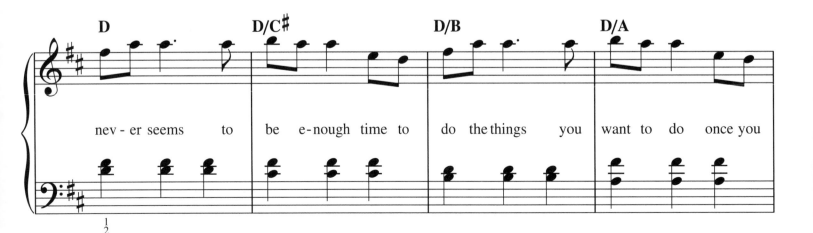

nev - er seems   to   be e-nough time to   do the things   you   want to do   once you

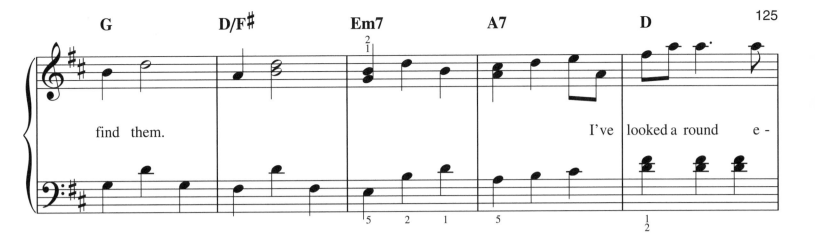

G   D/F#   Em7   A7   D

find them.   I've looked a round   e -

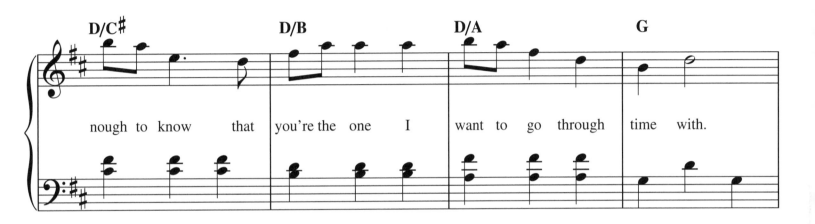

D/C#   D/B   D/A   G

nough to know   that   you're the one   I   want to go through   time with.

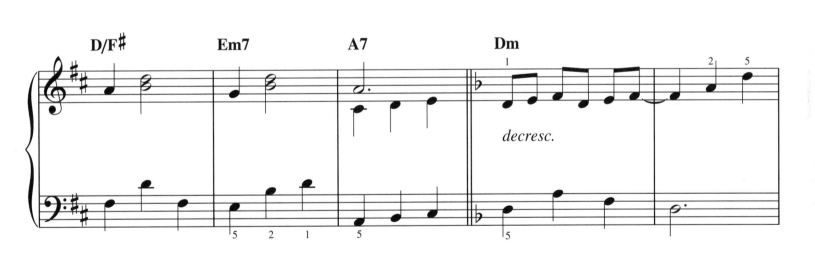

D/F#   Em7   A7   Dm

decresc.

pp

TEARS IN HEAVEN

Words and Music by ERIC CLAPTON
and WILL JENNINGS

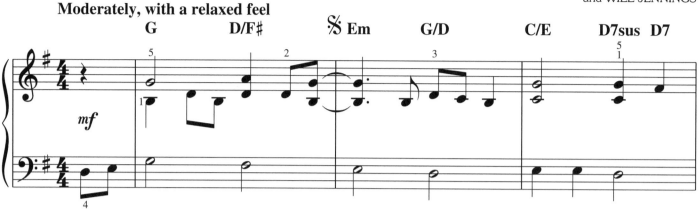

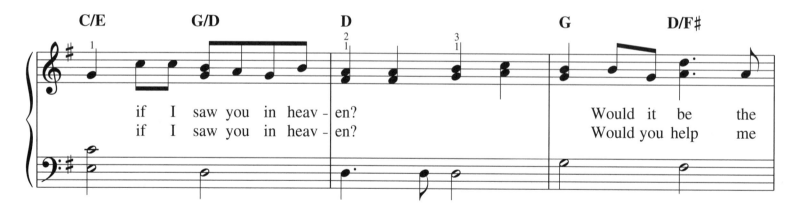

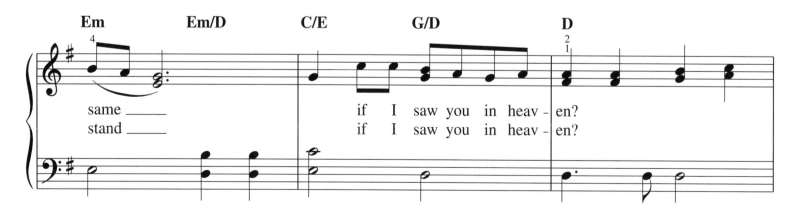

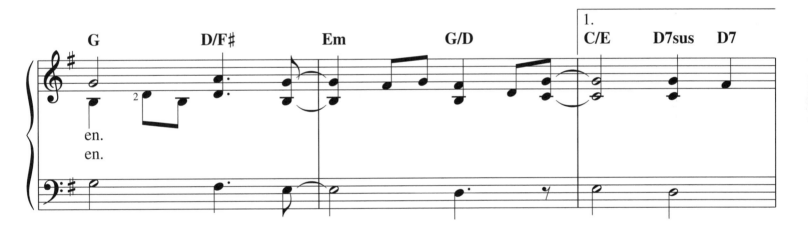

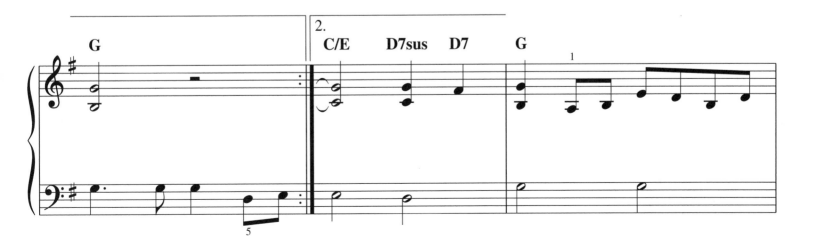

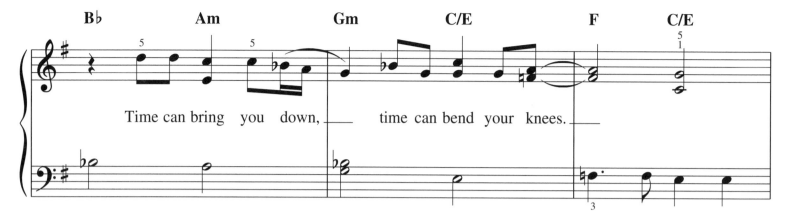

Time can bring you down,___ time can bend your knees.___

Time can break the heart,___ have you beg - gin' please,___

beg-gin' please.___ *(Instrumental)*

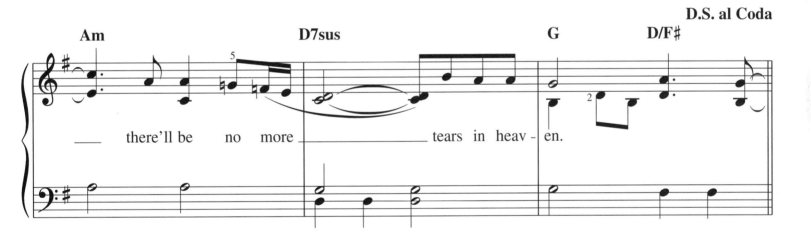

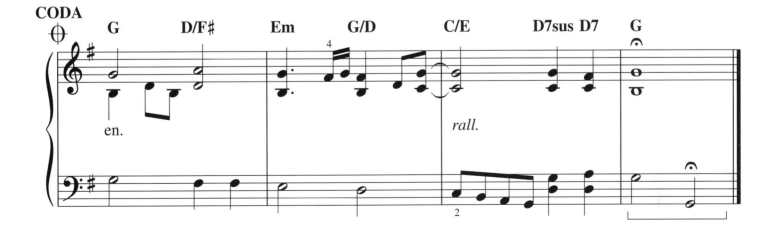

WANTED DEAD OR ALIVE

Words and Music by JON BON JOVI
and RICHIE SAMBORA

Moderately slow

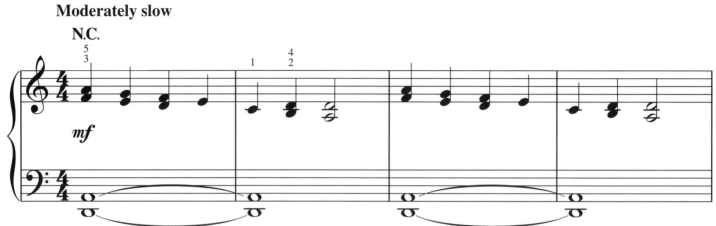

It's

all the same,
times I sleep,

on-ly the names will change, _____
some-times it's not for days, _____ and

ev - 'ry day, it seems we're wast - ing a - way.___ An -
peo -ple I meet al - ways go their sep -'rate ways. Some -

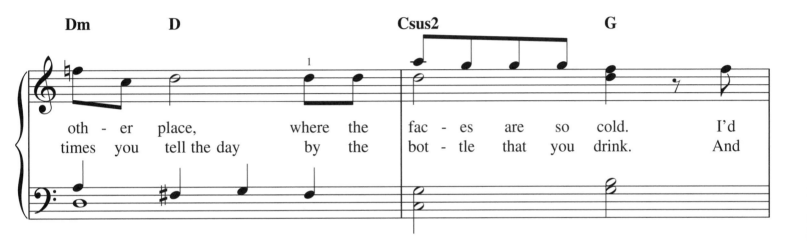

oth - er place, where the fac - es are so cold. I'd
times you tell the day by the bot - tle that you drink. And

drive all night,_____ just to get back___ home.___ } I'm a
times when you're_ a - lone,_____ all you do is think.__ }

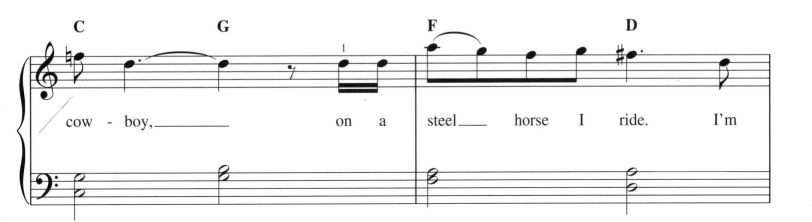

cow - boy,_____ on a steel___ horse I ride. I'm

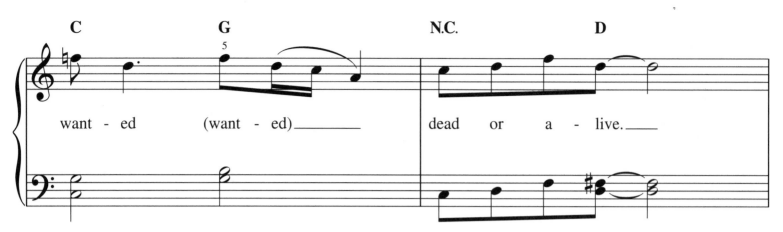

want - ed (want - ed)____ dead or a - live.____

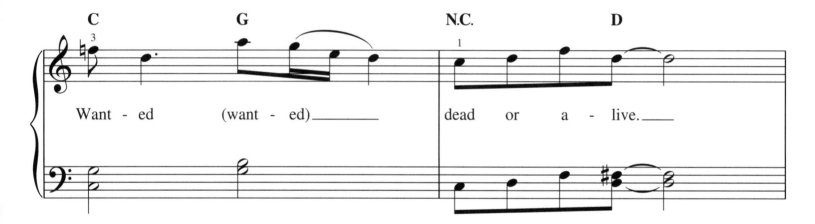

Want - ed (want - ed)____ dead or a - live.____

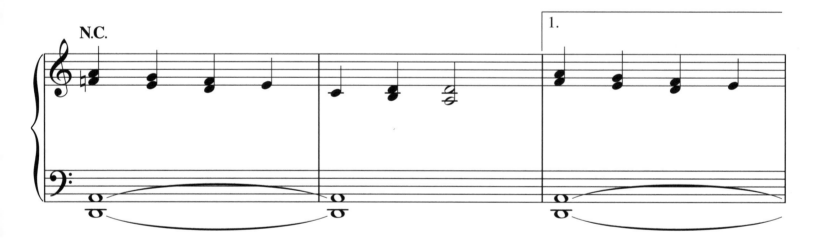

Some -

I'm a

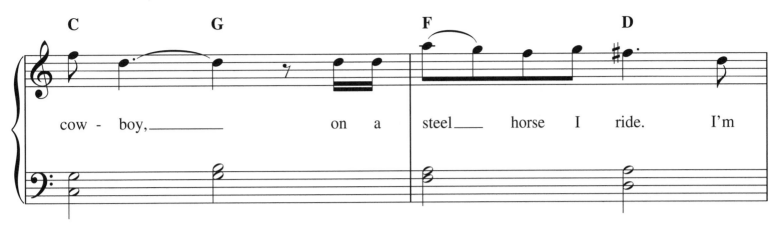

cow - boy,_____ on a steel___ horse I ride. I'm

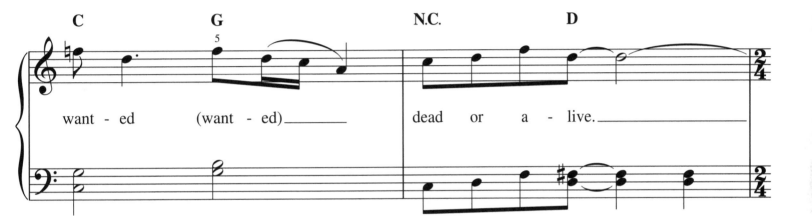

want - ed (want - ed)_____ dead or a - live._____

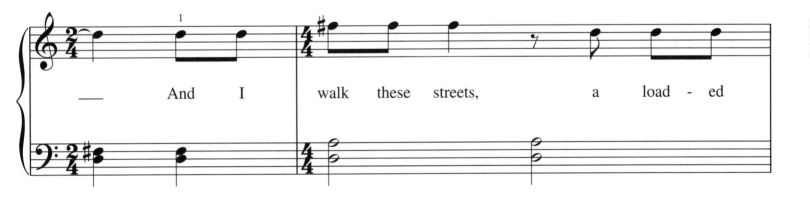

___ And I walk these streets, a load - ed

six - string on my back. I play for keeps, 'cause I

might not make it back._____ I been ev - 'ry - where,_____ still I'm

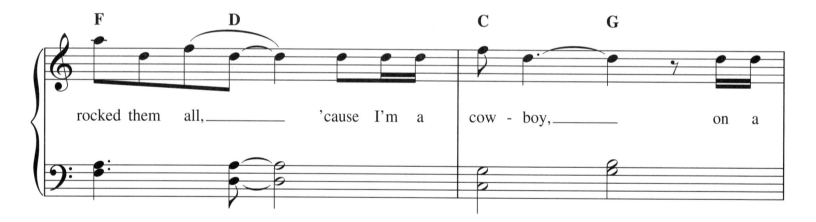

stand - ing tall._____ I've seen a mil - lion fac - es and I've

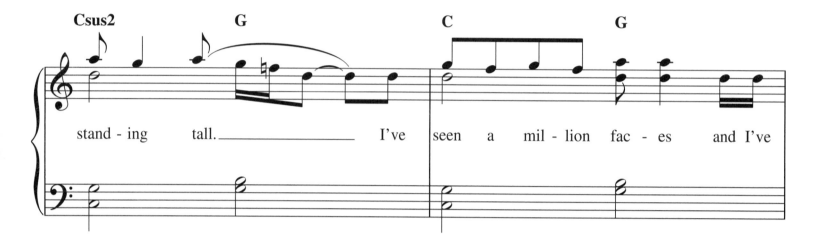

rocked them all,_____ 'cause I'm a cow - boy,_____ on a

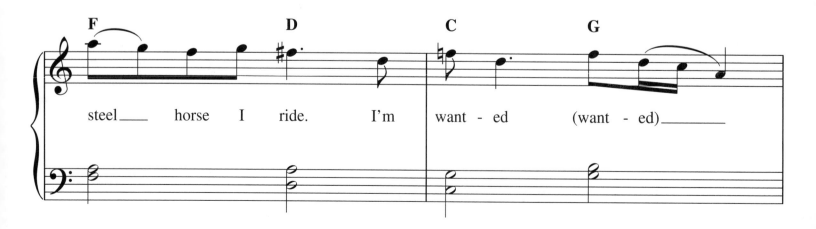

steel___ horse I ride. I'm want - ed (want - ed)_____

dead or a - live.___ Well, I'm a cow - boy._____ I got the

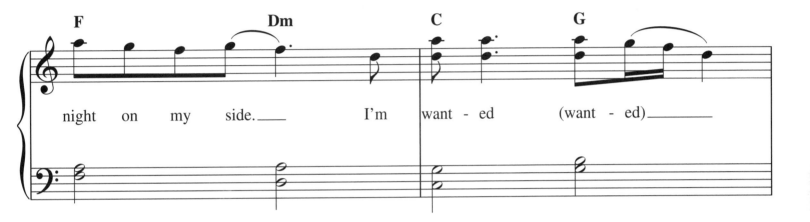

night on my side.___ I'm want - ed (want - ed)_____

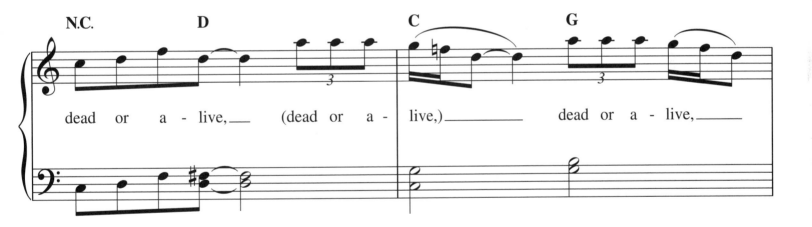

dead or a - live,___ (dead or a - live,)_____ dead or a - live,___

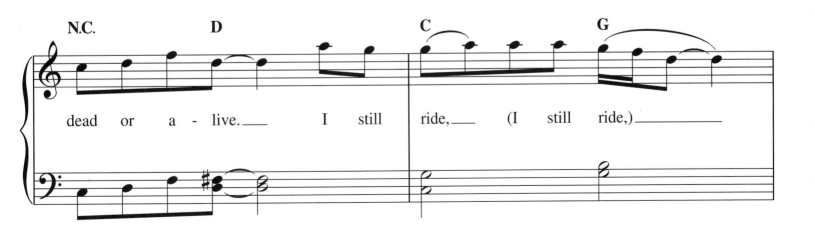

dead or a - live.___ I still ride,___ (I still ride,)_____

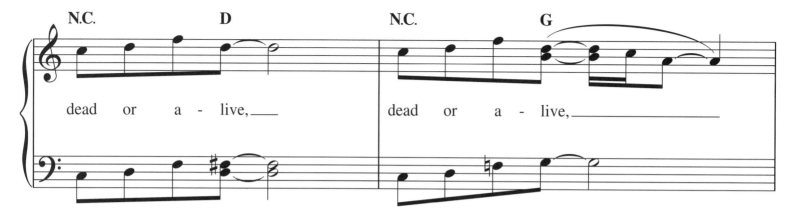

dead or a - live,____   dead or a - live,_____

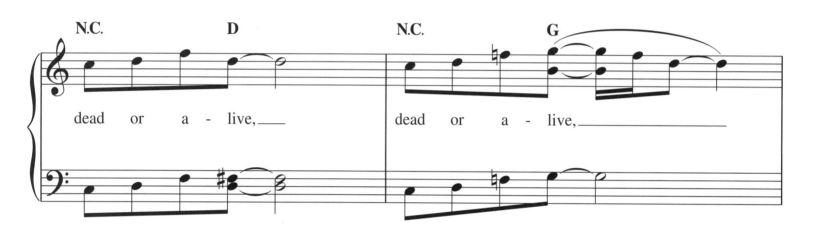

dead or a - live,____   dead or a - live,_____

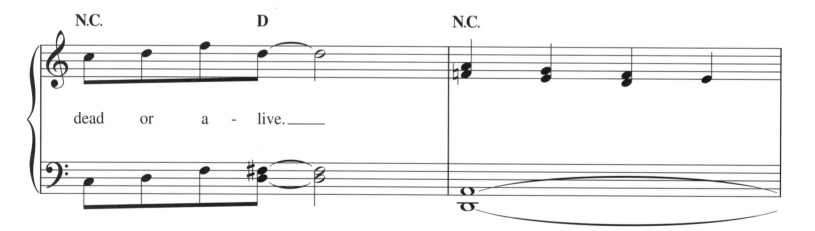

dead or a - live._____

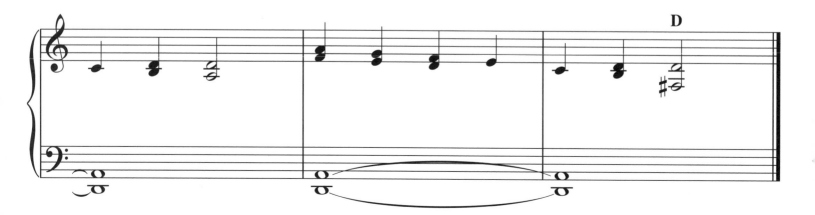

YOU'VE GOT A FRIEND

Words and Music by
CAROLE KING

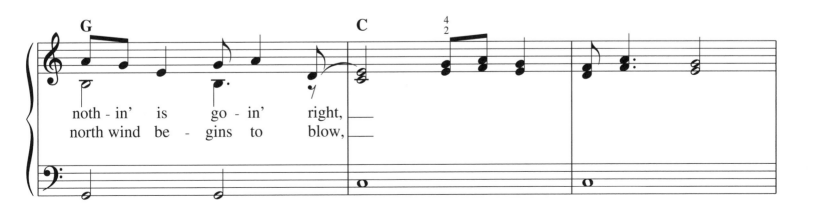

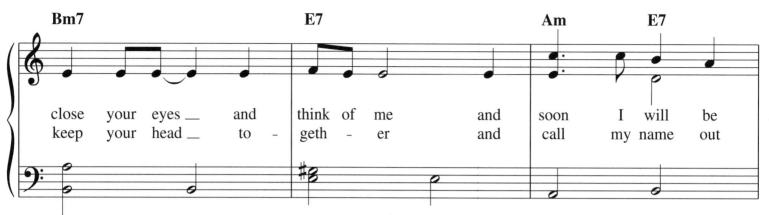

Bm7   E7   Am   E7

close your eyes __ and think of me and soon I will be
keep your head __ to - geth - er and call my name out

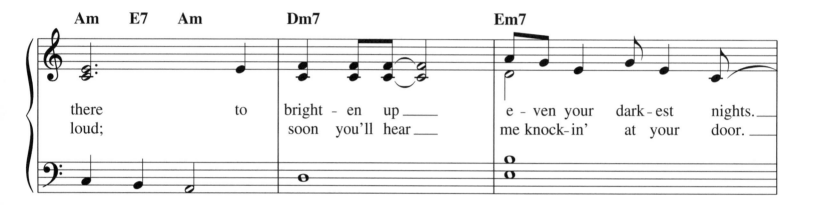

Am   E7   Am   Dm7   Em7

there   to bright - en up ___ e - ven your dark - est nights. ___
loud;   soon you'll hear ___ me knock-in' at your door. ___

F/G   G   F/G   % C

You just call out my ___ name ___

F

___ and you know wher - ev - er I am I'll come run -

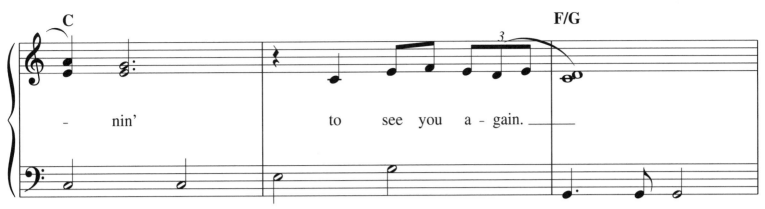

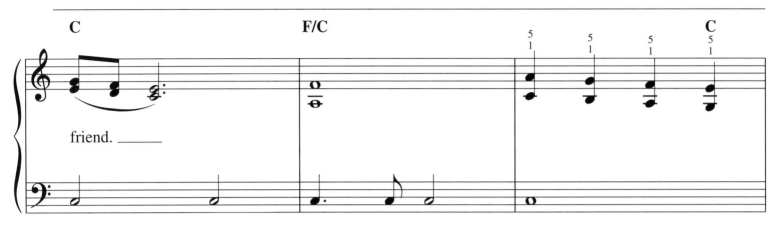

friend. _____

If the   be there, _____ yes,   I   will._____   Now

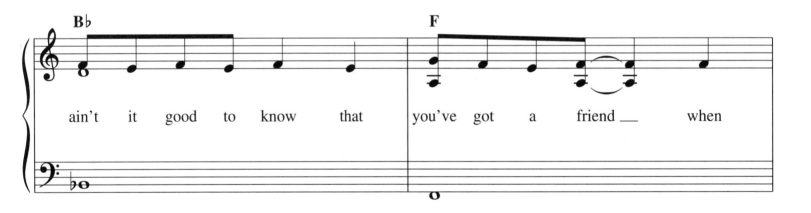

ain't   it   good   to   know   that   you've   got   a   friend ___   when

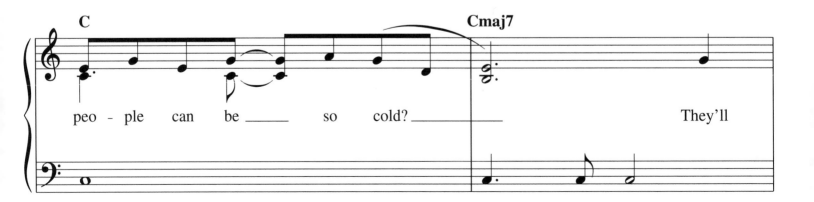

peo - ple   can   be _____   so   cold? _____ _____   They'll

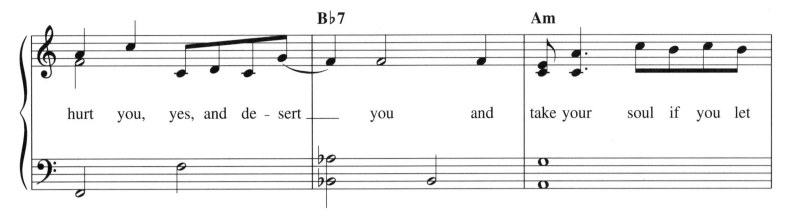

hurt you, yes, and de - sert ____ you and take your soul if you let

them. Oh, but don't you let ____ them. You just

D.S. al Coda

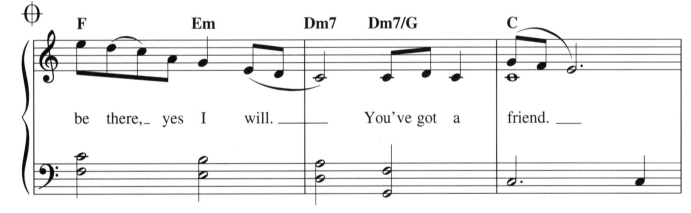

CODA

be there,_ yes I will. ____ You've got a friend. ____

Repeat and Fade

You've got a friend. ____ Ain't it good to know you've got a

YESTERDAY

Words and Music by JOHN LENNON
and PAUL McCARTNEY

Moderately, with expression

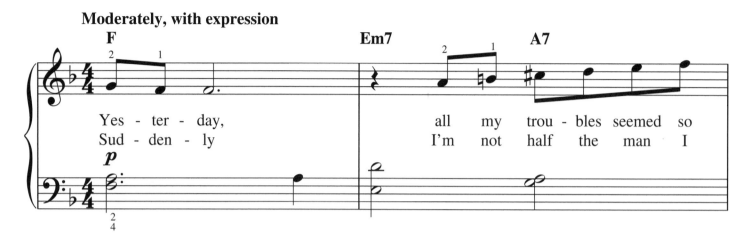

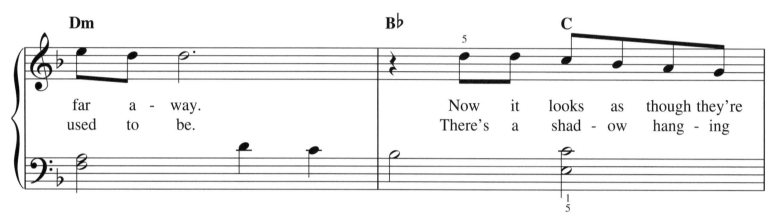

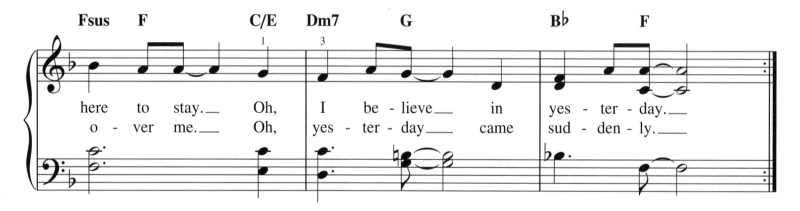

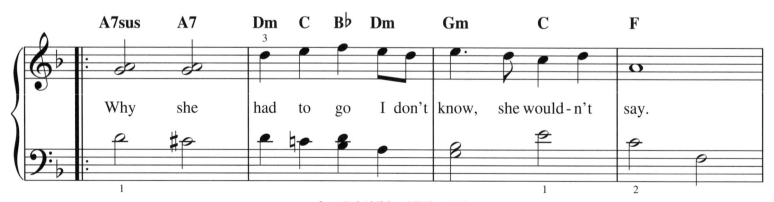

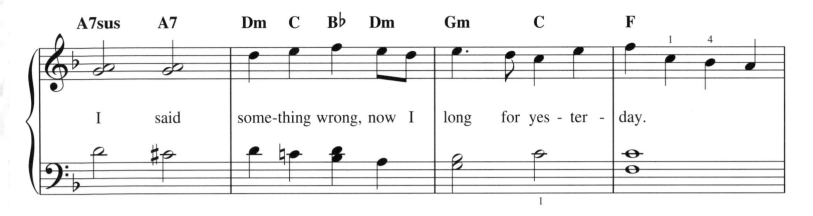

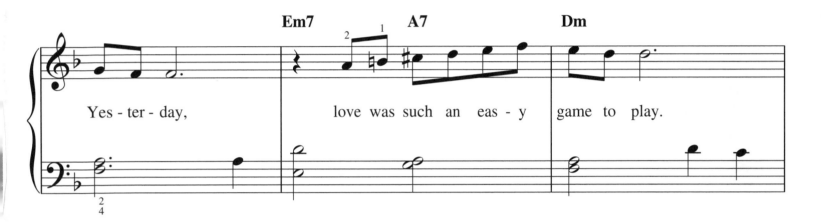

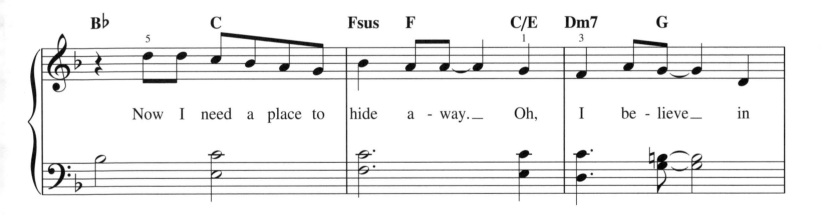

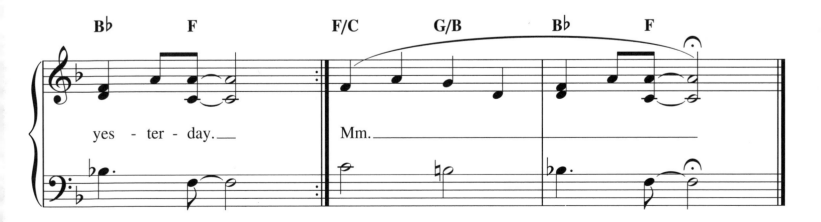

Preface

When I was studying at the Eastman School of Music, I didn't know which direction my career (if any) was going; probably the last thing in my imagination was that I might be a "popular" composer. I simply wanted to write good music.

It is still my life's ambition to do that—it's what my composition and theory teachers instilled in me—and I hope that any of you who use this book might notice (and maybe approve) the harmonies, rhythmic choices, and most importantly the richly talented collaborators that have come my way.

And if you sing any of these in the shower, I'll be particularly gratified.

Charles Strouse
June, 2008

Receiving his Bachelor of Music, 1947.

At the piano, circa 2003. Photo by Chuck Pulin.

The music of Charles Strouse

has touched the life of almost every American in the last half-century. There may be no other living composer from America's popular songbook whose work is as integrated into the popular culture as that of Charles Strouse.

His music has attracted top recording artists from the last half-century with covers of his songs recorded by such diverse pop artists as Barbra Streisand, Frank Sinatra, Tony Bennett, Bobby Darin, Harry Connick, Jr., Bobby Rydell, Jay-Z, Vic Damone, Louis Armstrong, Nina Simone, Grace Jones, and Duke Ellington and His Orchestra.

Strouse has written the scores to over 30 stage musicals, 14 scores for Broadway, four Hollywood films, two orchestral works, and two operas. He has been inducted to the Songwriter's Hall of Fame and the Theatre Hall of Fame. He is a three-time Tony® Award winner, a two-time Emmy® Award winner, and his cast recordings have earned him two GRAMMY Awards®. His song "Those Were the Days" launched over 200 episodes of the TV show "All in the Family" and continues to reach new generations of television audiences in syndication. With hundreds of productions licensed annually, his musicals *Annie* and *Bye Bye Birdie* are among the most popular musicals of all time produced by regional, amateur, and school groups all over the world.

Charles Strouse's first Broadway musical, *Bye Bye Birdie* (lyrics by Lee Adams), won a Tony® Award, as did *Applause*, starring Lauren Bacall, followed by *Annie* (also winner of two GRAMMYs). Other musicals include *All American* (book by Mel Brooks); *Golden Boy* (starring Sammy Davis, Jr.); *It's a Bird, It's a Plane, It's Superman*; *I and Albert* (London); *Dance a Little Closer* (lyrics by Alan Jay Lerner); *Charlie and Algernon* (Tony® nomination); *Rags* (Tony® nomination); and *Nick and Nora* (Tony® nomination). He wrote music and lyrics for *Mayor*, followed by the music for *Annie Warbucks*, the continuation of *Annie*.

Some of his film scores are *Bonnie & Clyde*, *The Night They Raided Minsky's*, and *All Dogs Go to Heaven*. "Born Too Late" (1958 pop song and top-10 *Billboard* hit for the Poni-Tails) and quadruple-platinum record "Hard Knock Life (Ghetto Anthem)," performed by artist Jay-Z, a GRAMMY winner for Best Rap Album of the Year and *Billboard's* R&B Album of the Year, reflect other aspects of his career which include orchestral works, chamber music, two piano concertos, and a pair of operas. In 2004 these operas, *The Future of the American Musical Theatre* (2004) and *Nightingale* (1985), were staged at the Eastman School of Music under the single title, *East Meets West*.

Strouse is a graduate of the Eastman School of Music, continuing his composition studies with Aaron Copland and Nadia Boulanger, founded the ASCAP Musical Theatre Workshop in New York (in which countless young composers and writers have found a forum for their work), and is the recipient of the "Richard Rodgers" as well as the "Oscar Hammerstein" Award. He is a member of the Theater Hall of Fame and the Songwriter's Hall of Fame. In 2005 he received the Dramatists' Guild Frederick Loewe Award and in 2008 he was honored by the Music Division of the Library of Congress.

Recent Charles Strouse releases include *Time-Life's Annie–The 30th Anniversary Cast Recording*. The most complete recording of the score to date, the double-disc features previously unrecorded material (including songs from *Annie 2*), a new overture by Strouse, and an all-star cast including Carol Burnett, Gary Beach, Kathie Lee Gifford, Andrea McArdle, Harve Presnell, John Schuck and Sally Struthers. In July 2008 Strouse's autobiography, *Put On a Happy Face*, was published by Sterling Publishing.

In January 2009 Strouse's *The Night They Raided Minsky's*, with lyrics by Susan Birkenhead (*Jelly's Last Jam*), a book by Bob Martin, and direction and choreography by Casey Nicholaw (both of *The Drowsy Chaperone*), premieres at The Ahmanson in Los Angeles. *Minsky's* is a big, racy, new musical comedy set in Prohibition Era New York City, recalling the free-spirited time of early showbiz comedians, con men, sexy chorus girls, hot music, and dancing. Other upcoming projects include two more musical adaptations of classic films: Paddy Chayevsky's *Marty* (to star Oscar-winner John C. Reilly) and Theodore Dreiser's *An American Tragedy*.

For more information about Charles Strouse and his upcoming events and appearances, visit **www.CharlesStrouse.com**.

Charles at the Eastman School of Music, circa 1947.

Charles being held by his mother at the beach, circa 1928.

Charles marries Barbara Siman, 1962.

The *Bye Bye Birdie* creative team: Director/Choreographer Gower Champion, Composer Charles Strouse, Producer Ed Padula, Book Writer Michael Stewart, and Lyricist Lee Adams, 1960.

Backstage at the Majestic Theatre, opening night of *Golden Boy*, 1964. Lyricist Lee Adams, Leading man Sammy Davis, Jr., and Charles.

Cast and creators of *Annie*, backstage at the Alvin Theatre, circa 1977. Book Writer Thomas Meehan, Lyricist/Director Martin Charnin, Andrea McArdle (Annie), Composer Charles Strouse, Reid Shelton (Daddy Warbucks), Musical Director Peter Howard, and Sandy.   Photo © Martha Swope.

Charles (left) with fellow songwriters Sammy Cahn, Sammy Fain, (unknown), (unknown), Jule Styne, Cy Coleman, (unknown), Hal David, (unknown). Seated are Jerry Lieber and Mike Stoller, circa 1980. Photo courtesy of the Charles Strouse Collection.

Charles (2nd from left) with collaborators Richard Maltby, Jr., Lee Adams, and Martin Charnin, circa 1991. Photo courtesy of the Charles Strouse Collection.

Annie reunion at the Paley Center for Media's tribute to Charles Strouse. Lyricist/Director Martin Charnin; Charles; the original Annie, Andrea McArdle; Book Writer Thomas Meehan, March, 2008. Photo by Philip Kessler.

Celebrating the launch of Charles' new book, June, 2008. Standing: Michael Feinstein, Sheldon Harnick and Stephen Schwartz. Seated: Lee Adams and Charles. Photo by Anita & Steve Shevett.

The Strouse family celebrates the launch of Charles' new book, June, 2008. Sons Will, Ben, and Nick, wife Barbara Siman, Charles, and daughter Victoria. Photo by Anita & Steve Shevett.

Charles Strouse
A Brief Essay by Ken Bloom

Once upon a time, in the first half of the last century, most popular songs came from Broadway and Hollywood. But with the rise of rock 'n' roll, it was rare that a song emerged from a dramatic context to capture the souls of listeners on records, radio and television.

That any pop hits emerged from Broadway amidst the rapidly lowering standards of songwriting was nothing less than a miracle. Few Broadway songwriters could achieve such success both on stage and off. Remarkably, Charles Strouse has written wonderful scores that have spawned immensely popular songs outside of the context of their shows. Just think about "Tomorrow" from his score for *Annie* and you've got the perfect example of the rare songwriting double play.

Strouse and his most regular scorewriting partner, Lee Adams, achieved success right off the bat with their first book show, *Bye Bye Birdie*. Imagine a first-time producer hiring a director/choreographer who has never staged a book musical, a first-time librettist, a first-time songwriting team, and a first-time star. Broadway is the most cynical of milieus and its denizens were not hopping with anticipation. But somehow Edward Padula, Gower Champion, Michael Stewart, Strouse and Adams, and Dick Van Dyke (not to mention Chita Rivera) surprised them all. And the new smash hit musical spawned a new smash hit song: "Put On a Happy Face." For their next outing, Strouse and Adams chose *All American*, a zany story of college life starring Ray Bolger, Eileen Herlie, Anita Gillette

and Ron Husmann. The libretto was by none other than Mel Brooks (he spoke of writing a musical titled *Springtime for Hitler* during the out-of-town tryout of the show). And, lo and behold, another hit emerged: "Once Upon a Time."

With two musical comedies under their collective belt, Strouse and Adams tried something darker— *Golden Boy*, with Sammy Davis, Jr. bringing his cyclonic energy to the stage. Even smart, sophisticated New York wasn't wholly prepared for an interracial love affair on Broadway. But despite bomb threats and bullet holes in the marquee of the Majestic Theatre, *Golden Boy* was a hit with a deeply felt, electric score by Strouse and Adams.

From the sublime to the ridiculous, the team turned to the comics for inspiration. Broadway genius Harold Prince produced and directed the camp classic, *It's a Bird, It's a Plane, It's Superman*. The show never caught on, despite the talents of Jack Cassidy and Linda Lavin and a kinetic score by the songwriting team. Though the show was presented in a pop art/tongue-in-cheek style, Strouse and Adams' score contained real heart, never condescending toward the characters. "You've Got Possibilities" came this close to becoming a true standard. Librettists Robert Benton and David Newman would later mine the same mother lode more successfully with the screenplay to *Superman: The Movie*. Historians often make excuses for favorite failures by proclaiming them ahead of their time. But *Superman* truly was a show ahead of the curve. Later, the hit television

CONTENTS (Alphabetical)

14	Applause	*Applause*
22	Baby, You Can Count on Me	*Bring Back Birdie*
17	Blame It on the Summer Night	*Rags*
26	Born Too Late	Recorded by the Poni-Tails
29	A Broadway Musical	*A Broadway Musical*
34	But Alive	*Applause*
42	Bye Bye Birdie	*Bye Bye Birdie*
46	Children of the Wind	*Rags*
37	Da-Da, Da-Da, Da, Da!	*Bojangles*
52	Dance a Little Closer	*Dance a Little Closer*
64	A Dancin' Man	*Bojangles*
68	Follow the Way of the Lord	*Bojangles*
72	For a Song to Be Beautiful	*Nightingale*
55	I Can't Stop Dancin'	*Can't Stop Dancin'*
76	I Don't Need Anything but You	*Annie*
81	I Want to Be with You	*Golden Boy*
84	It Would Have Been Wonderful	*Annie Warbucks*
92	It's the Hard-Knock Life	*Annie*
96	It's Time for You	Recorded by Frank Sinatra
89	Kids!	*Bye Bye Birdie*
100	Let's Make Music Together	*All Dogs Go to Heaven*
108	Let's Settle Down	*Bye Bye Birdie* (TV Version)
112	Look on the Bright Side	*Lyle the Crocodile*
105	Look Who's Alone Now	*Nick and Nora*
116	Lorna's Here	*Golden Boy*

122	A Lot of Livin' to Do	*Bye Bye Birdie*
128	Love	*Annie Warbucks*
119	Married Life	*Nick and Nora*
134	Maybe	*Annie*
137	My Star	*Marty*
147	N.Y.C.	*Annie*
142	Night Song	*Golden Boy*
150	No Man Is Worth It	*Dance a Little Closer*
154	Once Upon a Time	*All American*
158	One Boy (Girl)	*Bye Bye Birdie*
161	Pals	*Lyle the Crocodile*
164	Put On a Happy Face	*Bye Bye Birdie*
167	Saturday Night Girl	*Marty*
174	Smashing, New York Times	*Applause*
180	There's Always One You Can't Forget	*Dance a Little Closer*
184	There's Never Been Anything Like Us	*Dance a Little Closer*
177	This Is the Life	*Golden Boy*
192	Those Were the Days	*All in the Family* (TV Theme)
200	Tomorrow	*Annie*
195	Wanting	*Rags*
204	What Am I Gonna Do Without You?	The New *Golden Boy*
222	Whatever Time There Is	*Flowers for Algernon*
210	When You Smile	*Annie Warbucks*
214	You're Never Fully Dressed Without a Smile	*Annie*
218	You've Got Possibilities	*It's a Bird, It's a Plane, It's Superman*

APPLAUSE
from the Broadway Musical APPLAUSE

Lyric by LEE ADAMS
Music by CHARLES STROUSE

With a Rock beat

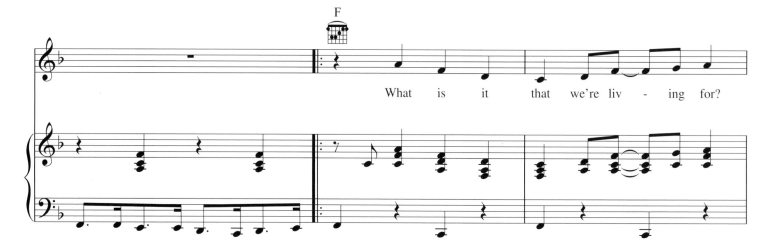

What is it that we're liv - ing for?

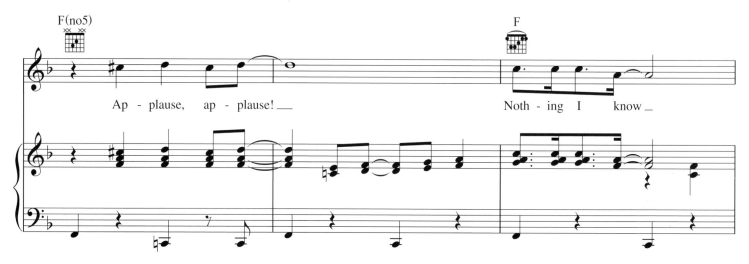

Ap - plause, ap - plause! __ Noth - ing I know __

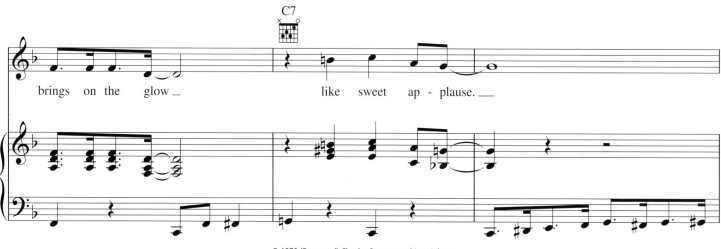

brings on the glow __ like sweet ap - plause. __

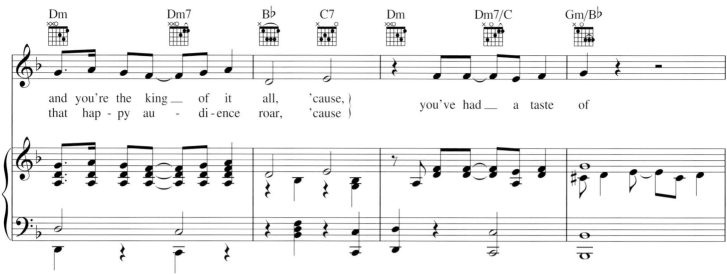

and you're the king __ of it all, 'cause, }
that hap-py au - di-ence roar, 'cause }
you've had __ a taste of

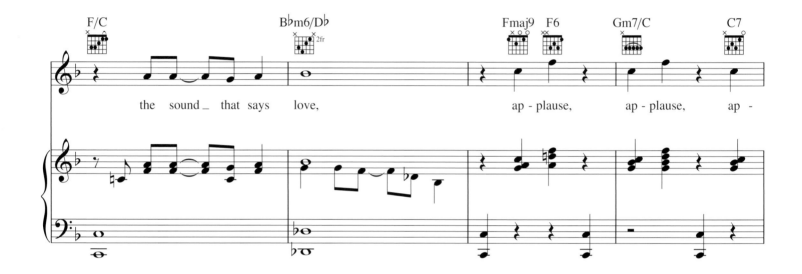

the sound __ that says love,
ap - plause, ap - plause, ap -

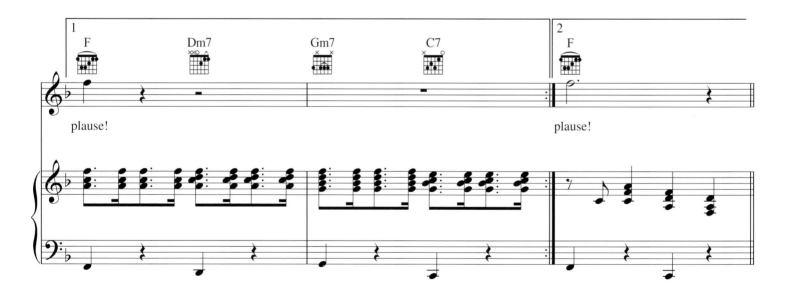

plause!

plause!

Repeat and Fade

BLAME IT ON THE SUMMER NIGHT

from RAGS

Lyric by STEPHEN SCHWARTZ
Music by CHARLES STROUSE

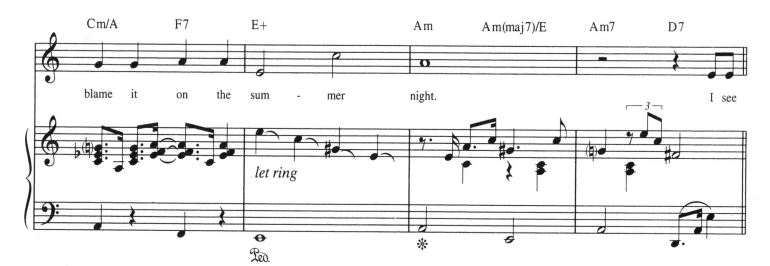

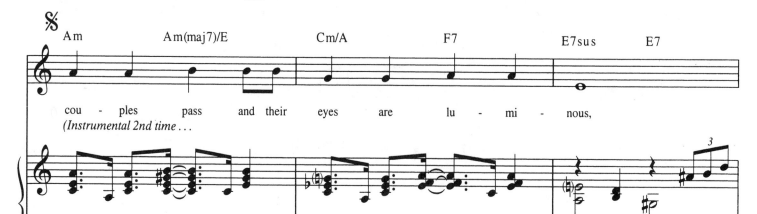

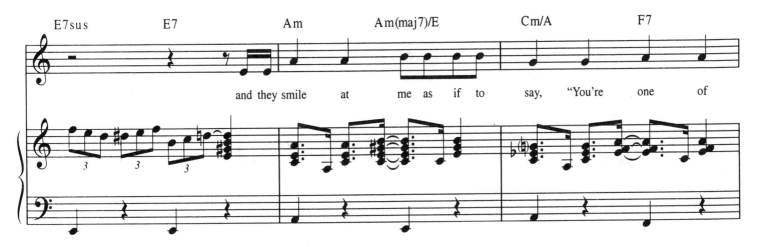

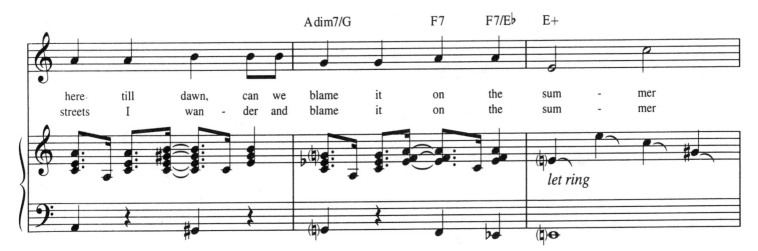

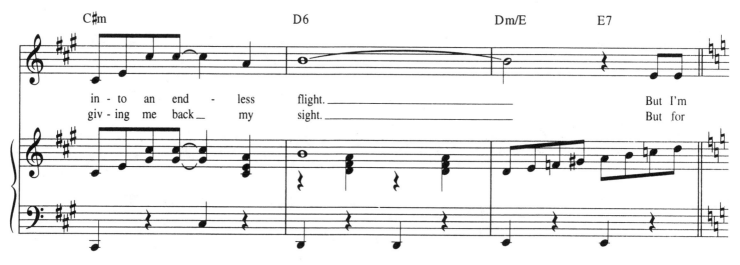

BABY, YOU CAN COUNT ON ME

from BRING BACK BIRDIE

Lyric by LEE ADAMS
Music by CHARLES STROUSE

Slowly and freely

1. So we're in the des - ert, so the sun is hot.
2. So you're hot and tired, so you're soak - ing wet.

So there ain't a soul a - round for miles and miles, so what? Hey, it could be
So we've lugged that lug - gage for two days and nights, and yet, things will bright - en

worse! And that ends the verse... The
for us. Now, the sec - ond cho - rus. You

Bet the whole a-mount___ on... Ba - by,

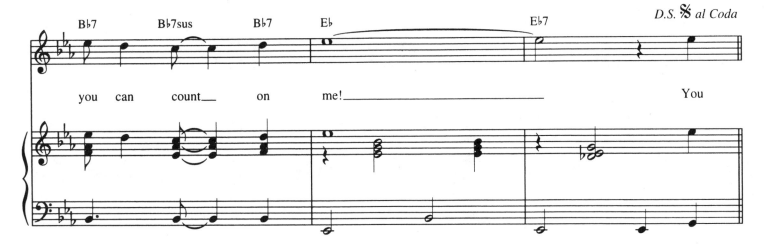

you can count___ on me!_____ You

D.S. % al Coda

⊕ *Coda*

Bet the whole a-mount___ on... Ba - by,

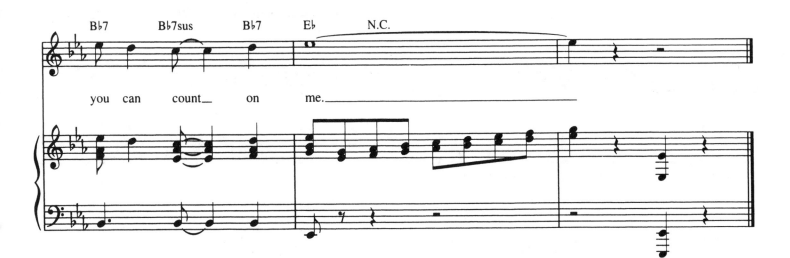

you can count___ on me._____

BORN TOO LATE

Lyric by FRED TOBIAS
Music by CHARLES STROUSE

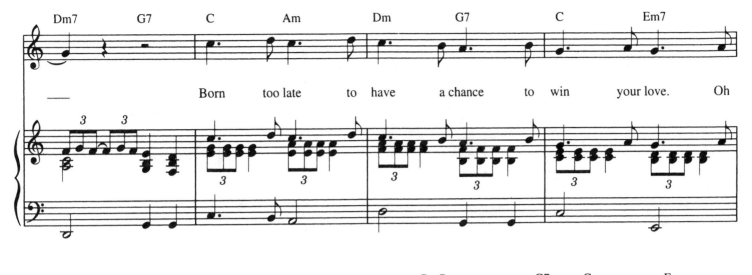

Born too late to have a chance to win your love. Oh

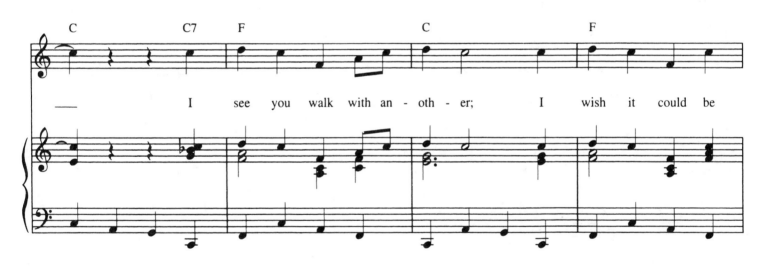

why, oh why was it my fate to be born too late?_____

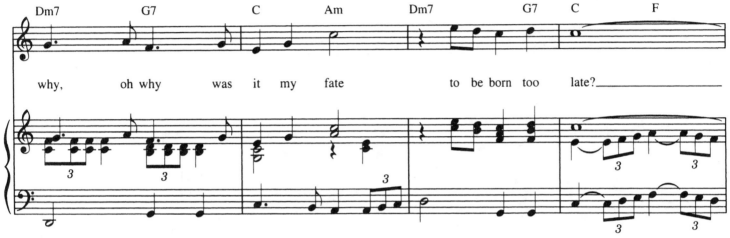

I see you walk with an-oth-er; I wish it could be

me; I long to hold you and kiss you, but I know it nev-er can

A BROADWAY MUSICAL
from A BROADWAY MUSICAL

Lyric by LEE ADAMS
Music by CHARLES STROUSE

funny scenes die, you wonder why____ you got

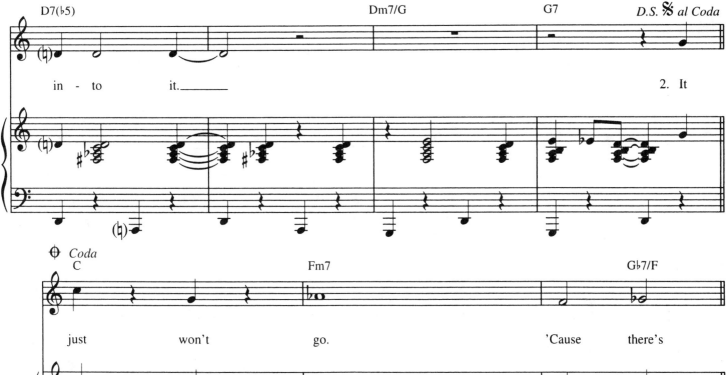

in - to it._____ 2. It

just won't go. 'Cause there's

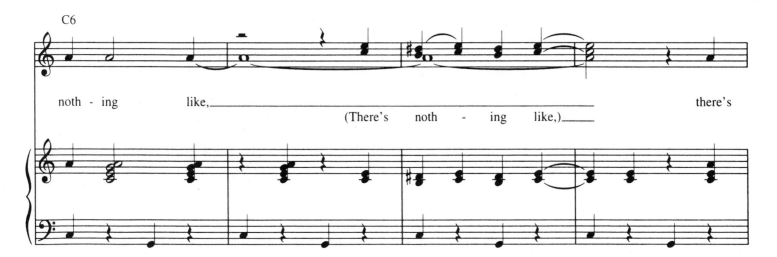

noth - ing like,____ there's
(There's noth - ing like,)____

noth-ing like a big brash._____ There's

noth-ing like a sas - sy, tune - ful, glam - o - rous

Broad - way_____ Mu - sic - al

show,_____

BUT ALIVE
from the Broadway Musical APPLAUSE

Lyric by LEE ADAMS
Music by CHARLES STROUSE

DA-DA, DA-DA, DA, DA!
from BOJANGLES

Lyric by SAMMY CAHN
Music by CHARLES STROUSE

Spoken: What does that mean? I'm gonna tell ya.

There is just no great-er sound_ than...

Makes my feet be - gin to pound...._

Don't play me no mel - o - dy_ like "Rhap-so - dy_ in Blue."_

BYE BYE BIRDIE

from BYE BYE BIRDIE

Lyric by LEE ADAMS
Music by CHARLES STROUSE

why'd ya have to go? _____
till you're home to

stay. _____ I'll

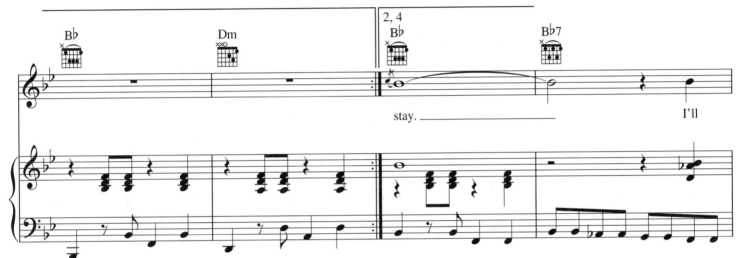

miss the way you smile, as though it's just for

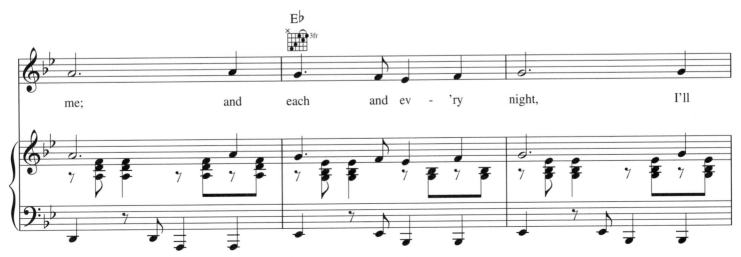

me; and each and ev-'ry night, I'll

write you faith - ful - ly! _____

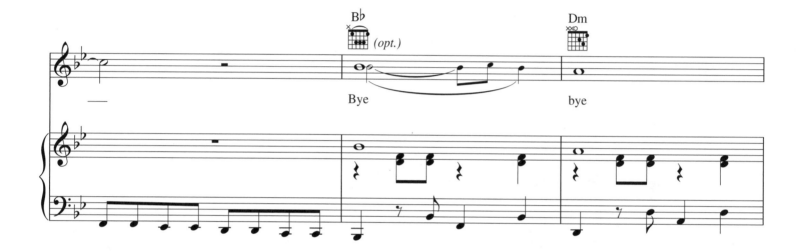

_ Bye bye

Bird - ie, it's

aw - ful hard to bear. _____

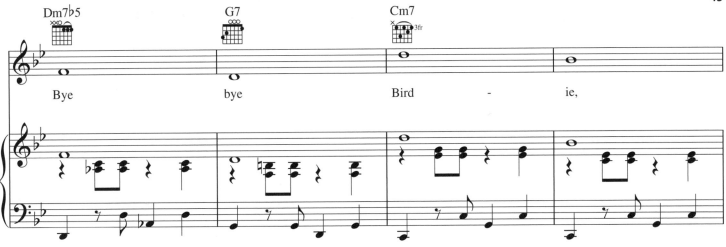

Bye bye Bird - ie,

guess I'll al - ways care.

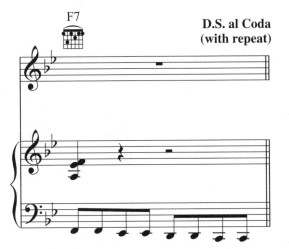

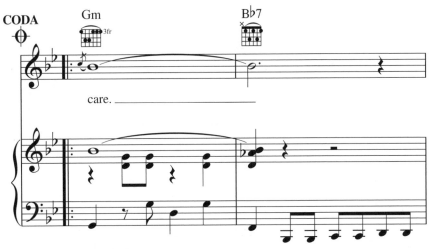

care.

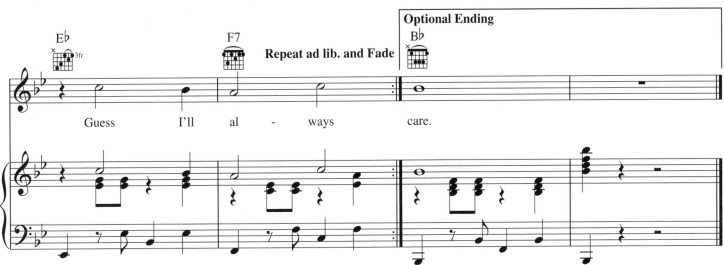

Guess I'll al - ways care.

CHILDREN OF THE WIND

from RAGS

Lyric by STEPHEN SCHWARTZ
Music by CHARLES STROUSE

for a life - time. And I'll know then they will nev - er

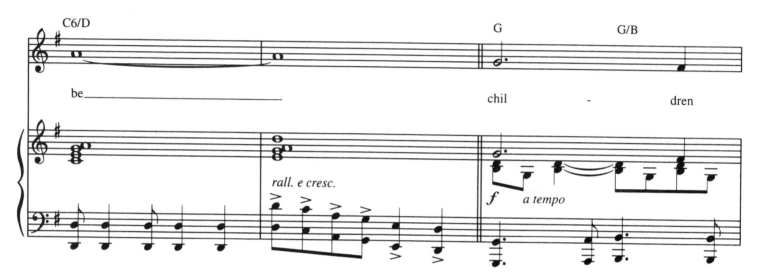

be_____ chil - dren

of the wind, long - ing to be one

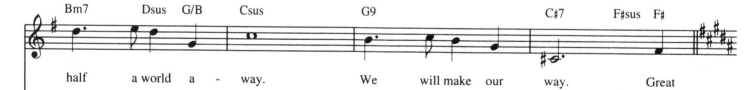

half a world a - way. We will make our way. Great

DANCE A LITTLE CLOSER

from DANCE A LITTLE CLOSER

Lyric by ALAN JAY LERNER
Music by CHARLES STROUSE

I CAN'T STOP DANCIN'

from CAN'T STOP DANCIN'

Words and Music by
CHARLES STROUSE

But my friend, soon you will.__ Tell me this: Did you

hate your moth-er?__ *Ah ha!* Well, you must take this pill."__ Then he

sent me this bill,__ but I still_____ can't stand still._____

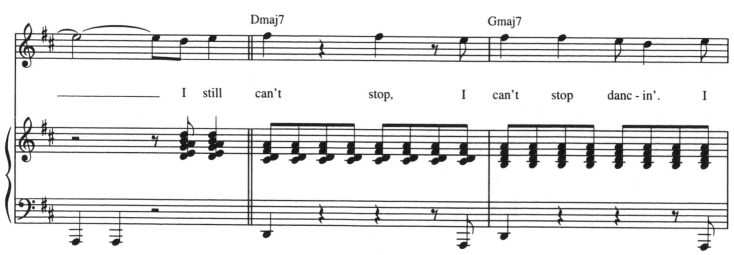

_____ I still can't stop, I can't stop danc-in'. I

can't   stop,   I   can't   stop   danc - in'.

Whoa   whoa whoa   whoa   whoa   whoa   whoa.

I   bought a   big   dog.   Now,   He's

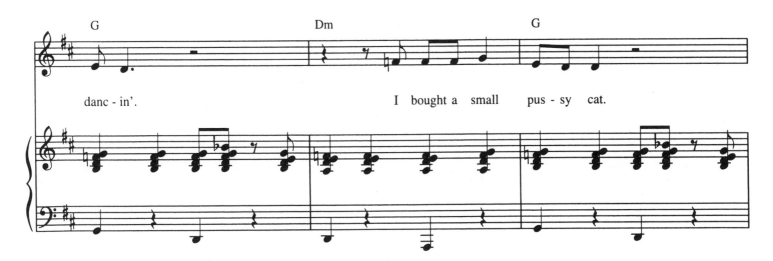

danc - in'.   I   bought a   small   pus - sy   cat.

Now, she's danc - in'. I chained my - self to my kitch-en sink.

But what do you think:__ We went out danc - in',

me and my sink.__ (Least I did - n't need to drink.) I tried

slow mu - sic, I tried no

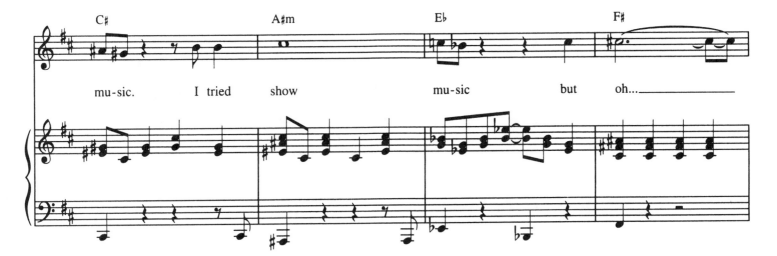

mu-sic. I tried show mu-sic but oh...._____

Whoa_____ I can't stop, I

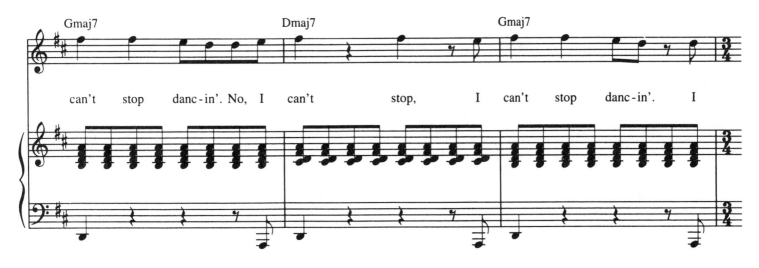

can't stop danc-in'. No, I can't stop, I can't stop danc-in'. I

can't stop____ danc - in'____ now!

ballet like

One day at dance class I was told__ 'bout this

In - di - an gu - ru, ve - ry old,__ who lived on a moun - tain

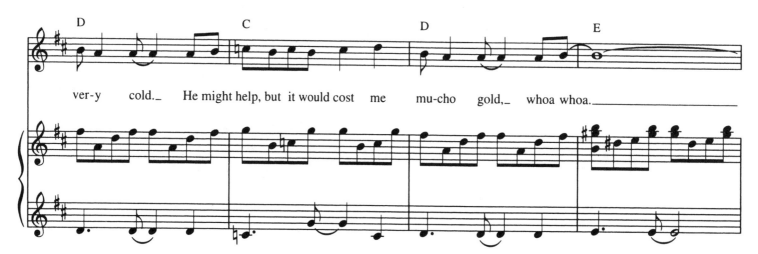

ver-y cold._ He might help, but it would cost me mu-cho gold,_ whoa whoa._____

Rubato

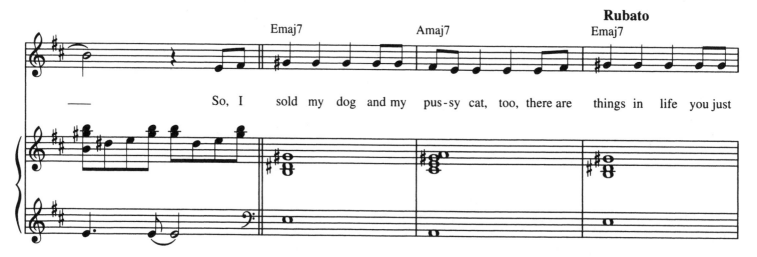

— So, I sold my dog and my pus-sy cat, too, there are things in life you just

got to do.__ *Good - bye!* And now I danced 'cross

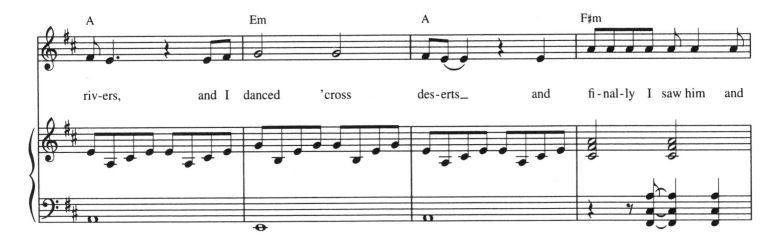

riv-ers, and I danced 'cross des-erts__ and fi-nal-ly I saw him and

like they said, man, he was so old he was al-most dead.__ And I start-ed to speak, but he

held up his hand.__ He said, "My son, I think I un-der-stand,__ you can't stop, you

A DANCIN' MAN
from BOJANGLES

Lyric by SAMMY CAHN
Music by CHARLES STROUSE

Moderately

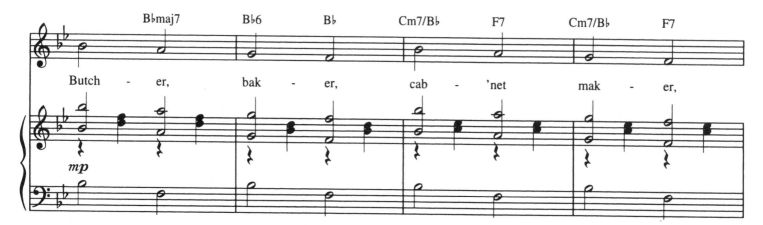

Butch - er, bak - er, cab - 'net mak - er,

law - yer, gro - cer; I say, "No Sir."

A danc - in' man, _____ a danc - in' man _____ I al - ways

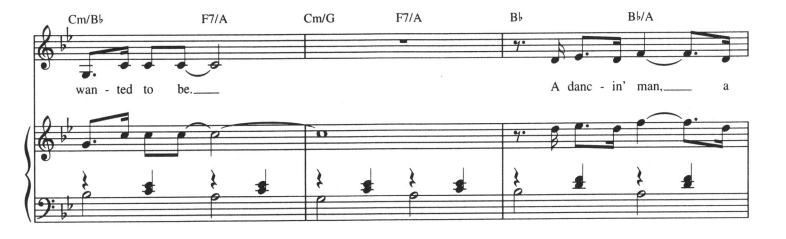

wan - ted to be._____ A danc - in' man,_____ a

danc - in' man;_____ the bill - ing fits per-fect - ly._____

I_____ got to dance or die,_____ I mean
Gee,_____ play some jazz for me_____ and you'll

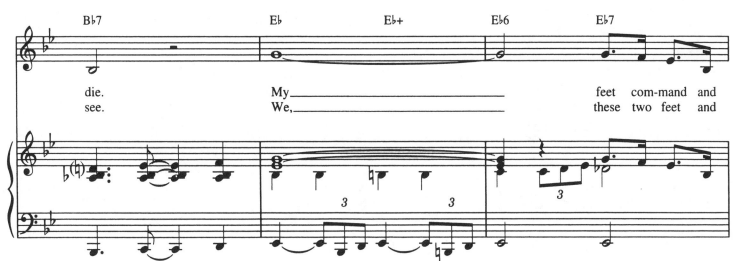

die.   My_____ feet com-mand and
see.   We,_____ these two feet and

FOLLOW THE WAY OF THE LORD
from BOJANGLES

Lyric by SAMMY CAHN
Music by CHARLES STROUSE

FOR A SONG TO BE BEAUTIFUL

from NIGHTINGALE

Words and Music by
CHARLES STROUSE

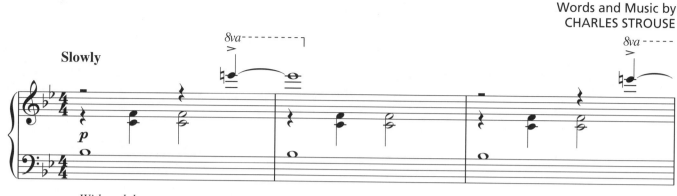

Slowly

With pedal

For a song to be beau-ti-ful, __ an art-ist must be free. For a

song to be beau-ti-ful, __ an art-ist must be free. __ Free __ to

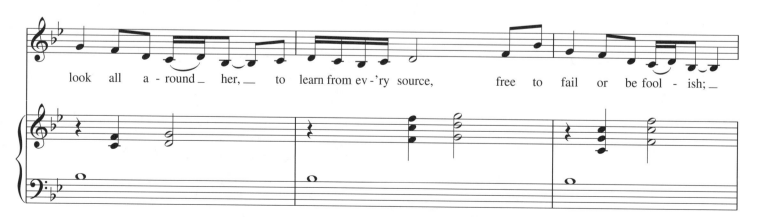

look all a-round __ her, __ to learn from ev-'ry source, free to fail or be fool-ish; __

e - ven that, of course. Can't you

see, can't you see that for a

song to be beau - ti - ful, an art - ist must be

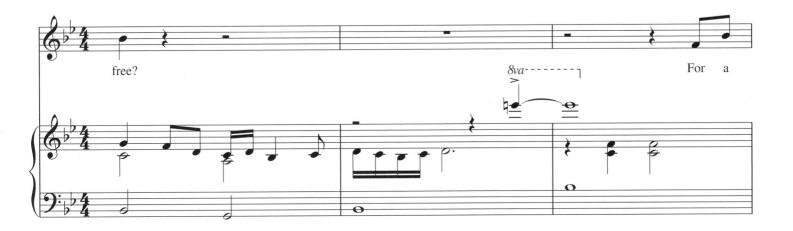

free? For a

child to be-come a man, the whole world he must see. For a

flow'r to be nour-ished it must wel-come ev-'ry bee. And

I must be free to fly, make my own mis-takes; that is what it takes.

cresc.

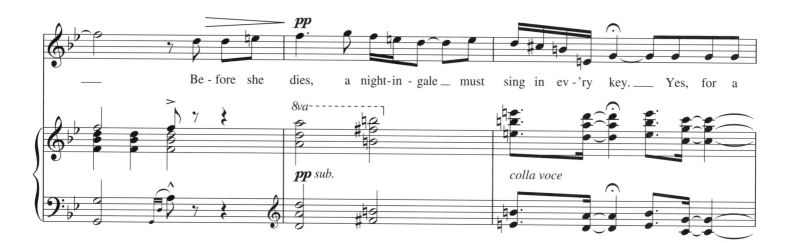

Be-fore she dies, a night-in-gale must sing in ev-'ry key. Yes, for a

pp sub.

colla voce

song to be beau-ti-ful, _____ an art-ist must _____ be

free.

For a

song to be beau-ti-ful, _ an art-ist must be... An art-ist must be... free.

I DON'T NEED ANYTHING BUT YOU

from the Musical Production ANNIE

Lyric by MARTIN CHARNIN
Music by CHARLES STROUSE

To - geth - er at last, / Cole Por - ter needs praise   to - geth - er for - ev - er; / in or - der to write more;

we're ty - ing a knot / Lu - go - si needs teeth   they nev - er can sev - er. / the bet - ter to bite more.

78

I WANT TO BE WITH YOU

from GOLDEN BOY

Lyric by LEE ADAMS
Music by CHARLES STROUSE

IT WOULD HAVE BEEN WONDERFUL

from ANNIE WARBUCKS

Lyric by MARTIN CHARNIN
Music by CHARLES STROUSE

Moderately

It would have been

won - der - ful,_____ just giv - en the chance.
char - ac - ter,_____ it would have had spine.

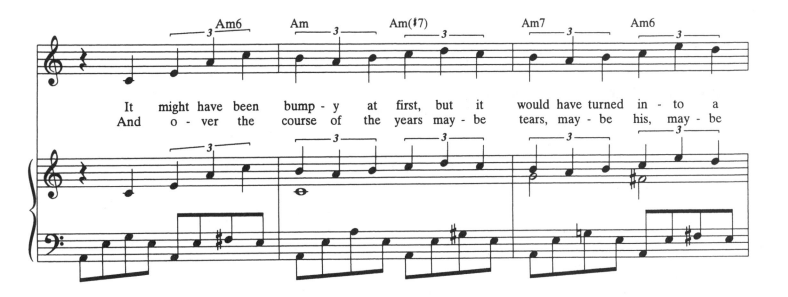

It might have been bump-y at first, but it would have turned in-to a
And o-ver the course of the years may-be tears, may-be his, may-be

dance._____ A mir-a-cle thing, like the spring as you
mine._____ It would have meant work, love needs work, or it's

feel new be-gin-nings be-gin._____ On - ly
no long-er love that you're in._____ Oh, but

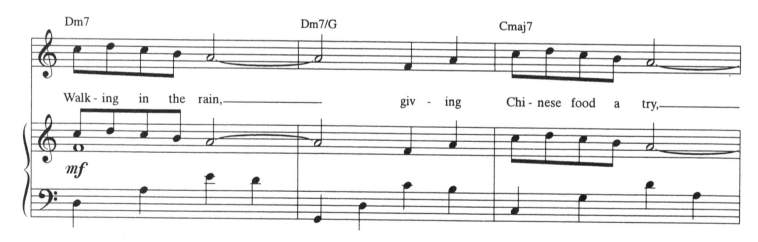

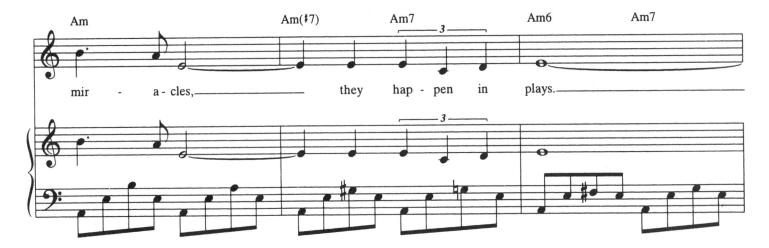

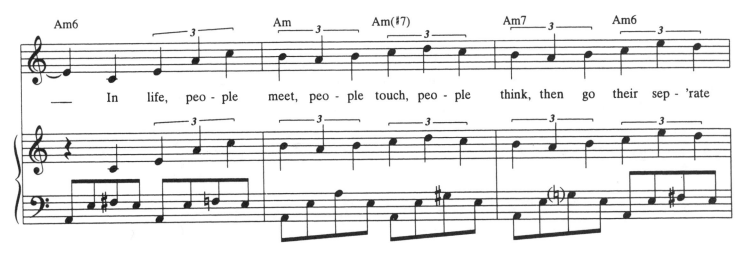

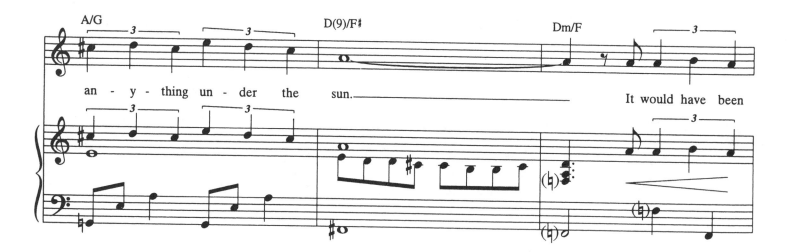

an - y - thing un - der the sun._____ It would have been

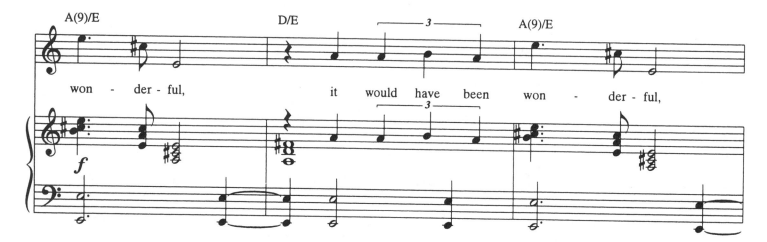

won - der - ful, it would have been won - der - ful,

it would have been won - der - ful, had it on - ly be -

gun._____

KIDS!
from BYE BYE BIRDIE

Lyric by LEE ADAMS
Music by CHARLES STROUSE

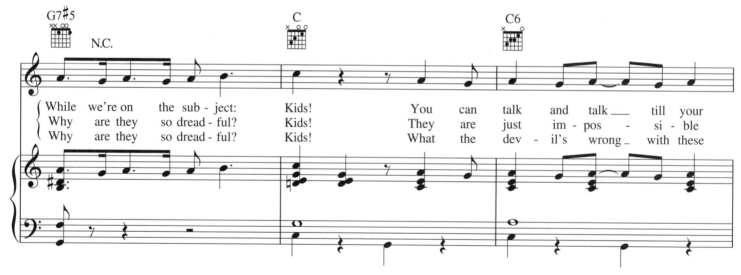

IT'S THE HARD-KNOCK LIFE

from the Musical Production ANNIE

Lyric by MARTIN CHARNIN
Music by CHARLES STROUSE

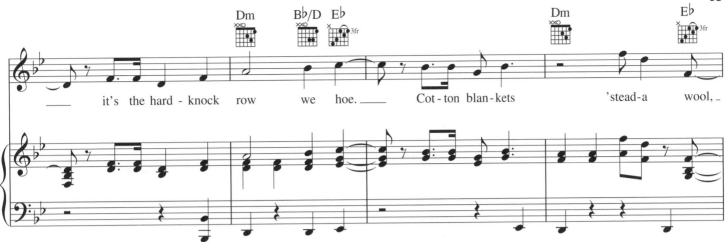

it's the hard-knock row we hoe. ___ Cot-ton blan-kets 'stead-a wool, ___

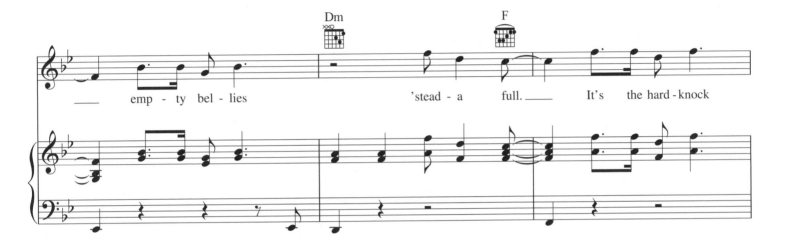

___ emp-ty bel-lies 'stead-a full. ___ It's the hard-knock

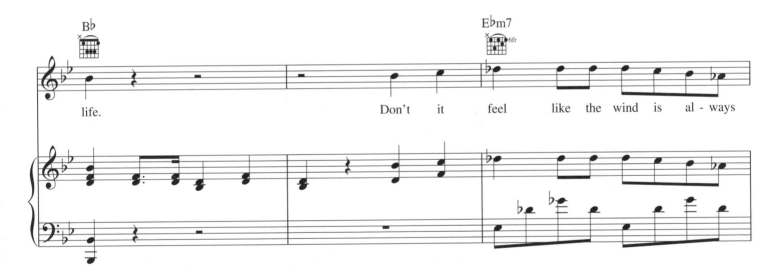

life. Don't it feel like the wind is al-ways

howl-in'? Don't it seem like there's nev-er an-y light? Once a

IT'S TIME FOR YOU

Lyric by SAMMY CAHN
Music by CHARLES STROUSE

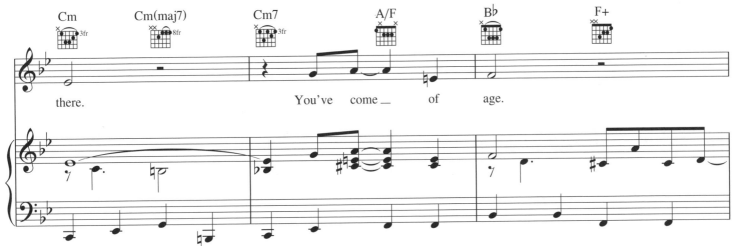

there. You've come ___ of age.

So man-y plac-es to be, ___ fac-es to see; ___

break out ___ of that cage! What I'm say-in' is, don't just

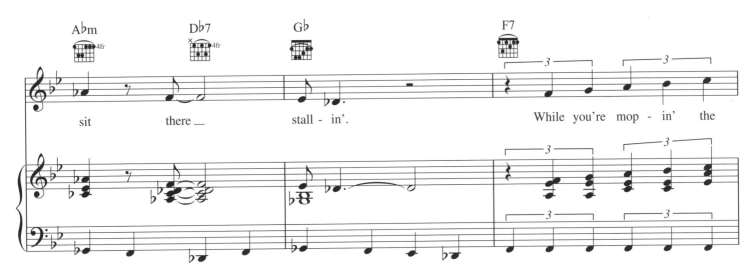

sit there ___ stall-in'. While you're mop-in' the

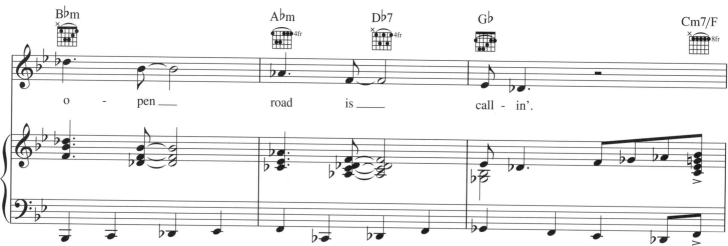

o - pen ___ road is ___ call - in'.

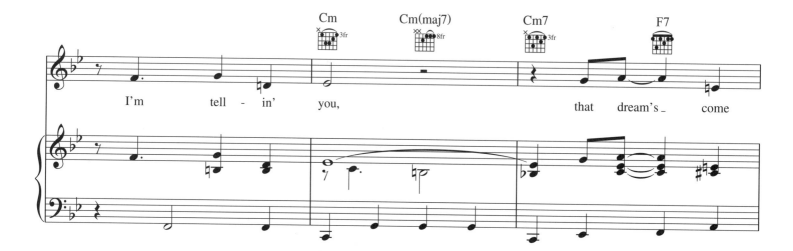

I'm tell - in' you, that dream's _ come

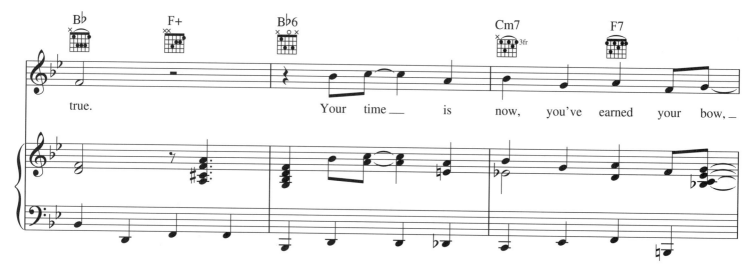

true. Your time ___ is now, you've earned your bow, _

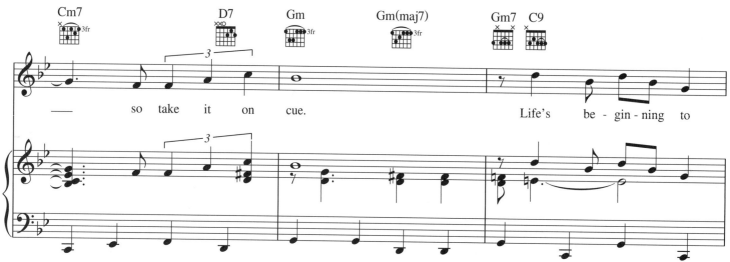

___ so take it on cue. Life's be - gin - ning to

rhyme. Get off __ of that dime. Come on, ba - by, it's

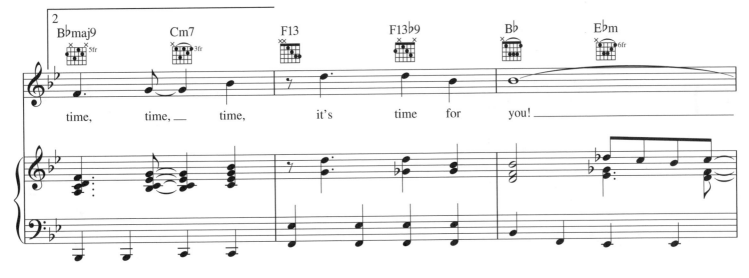

1

time, it's time for you!

2

time, time, __ time, it's time for you! _____

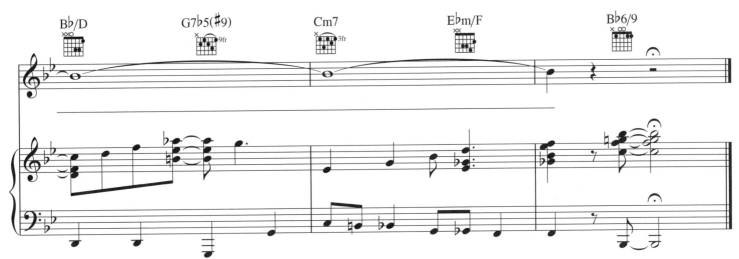

LET'S MAKE MUSIC TOGETHER

from ALL DOGS GO TO HEAVEN

Words and Music by
CHARLES STROUSE

life was nev-er to-geth - er, then we found the right key.___

___ Yeah,___ now we're birds___ of a feath - er,

Tweet, tweet, tweet.

fly - ing high___ on a sweet mel - o - dy. It's a per - fect

night for a song. Come a - long,___ let the mu - sic's nat - u - ral beat

move your feet.___ But if you still feel that old doubt,_ let___ the breath out___ and

sing. Oh,_____ oh,_____ oh,_____ oh._____

There is noth-ing like sing — ing when the har-mo-ny blends._____

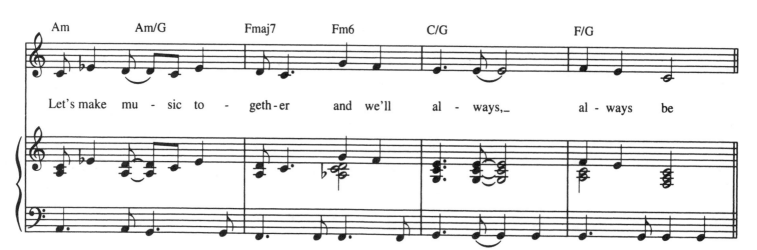

Let's make mu - sic to - geth-er and we'll al - ways,_ al - ways be

LOOK WHO'S ALONE NOW

from NICK AND NORA

Lyric by RICHARD MALTBY, JR.
Music by CHARLES STROUSE

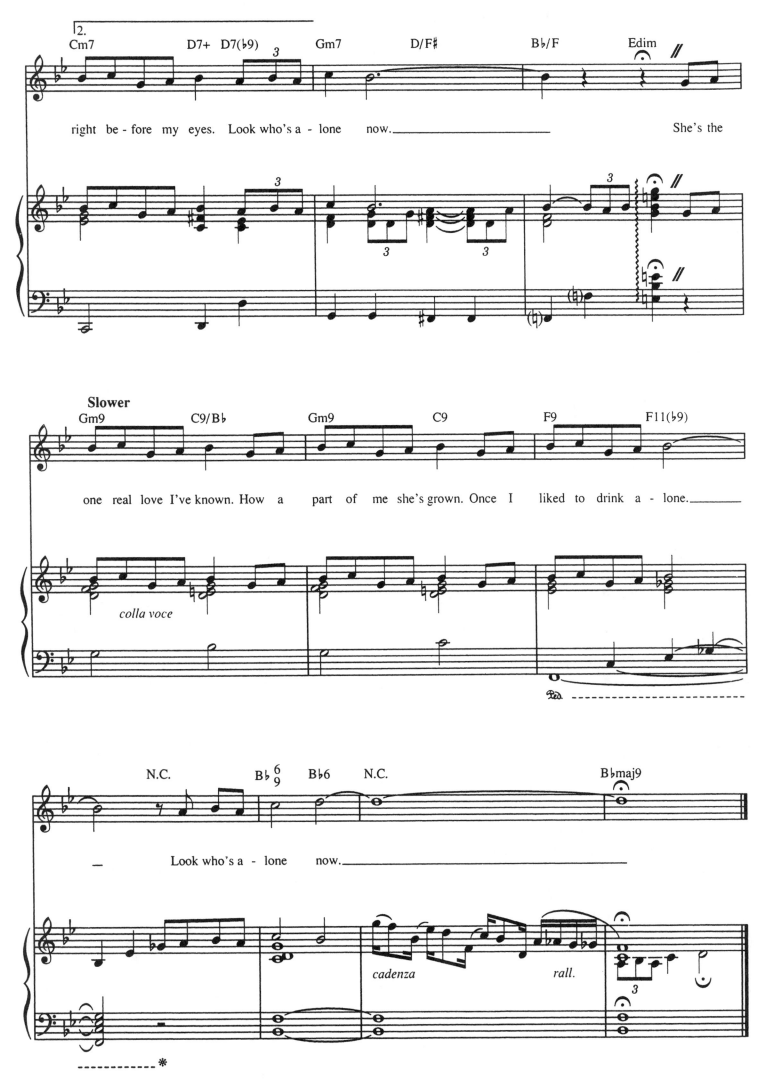

LET'S SETTLE DOWN
from BYE BYE BIRDIE

Lyric by LEE ADAMS
Music by CHARLES STROUSE

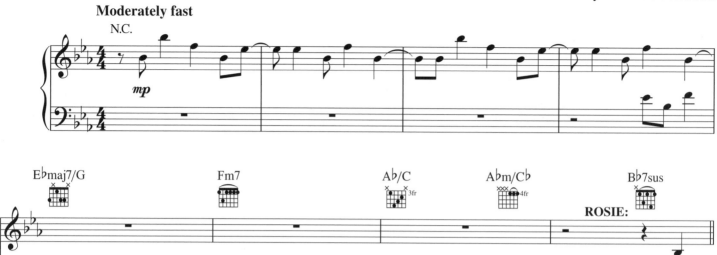

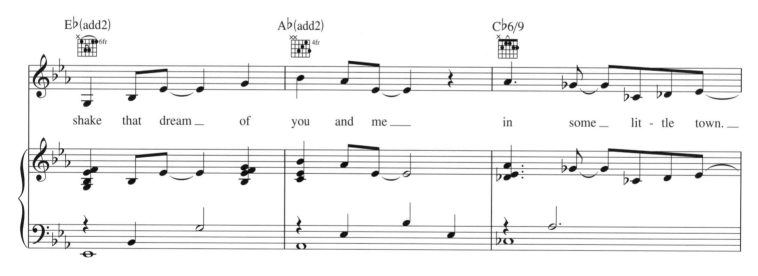

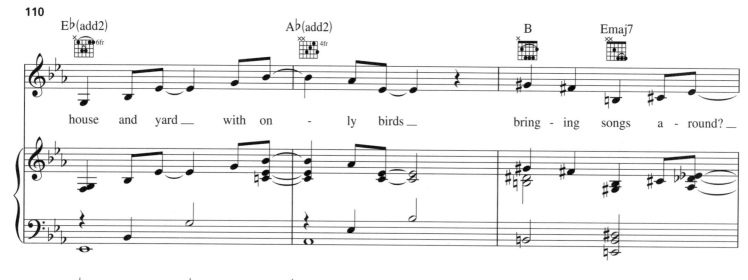

house and yard ___ with on - ly birds ___ bring - ing songs a - round? ___

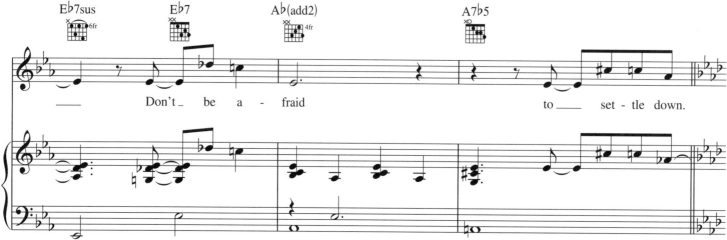

___ Don't ___ be a - fraid to ___ set - tle down.

That ___ green stuff's grass, and ___ that smell ev - 'ry - where,

know what that is? ___ Fresh air. ___

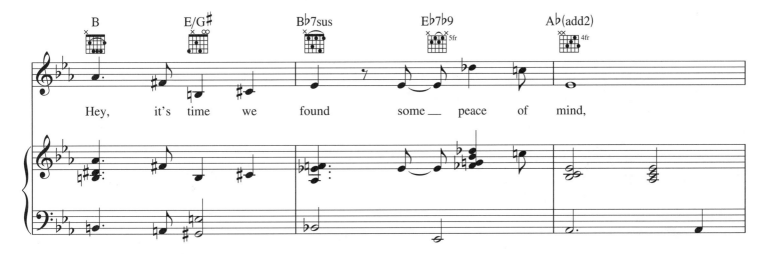

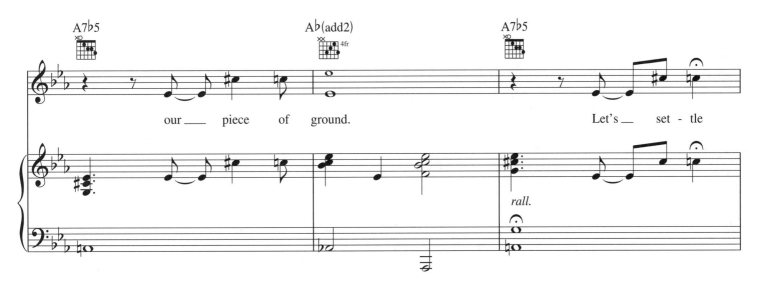

LOOK ON THE BRIGHT SIDE

from LYLE THE CROCODILE

Words and Music by
CHARLES STROUSE

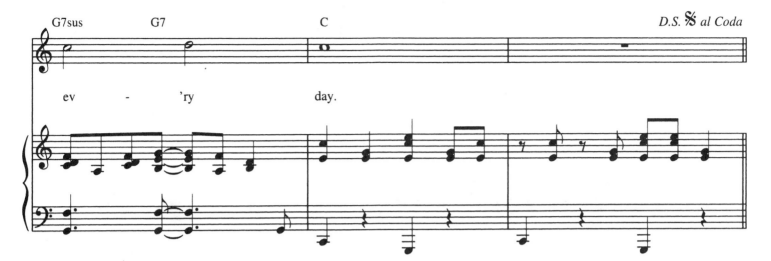

ev - 'ry day.

D.S. 𝄋 al Coda

𝄌 *Coda*

ev - 'ry, turn - ing ev - 'ry,

turn - ing ev - 'ry day!_____

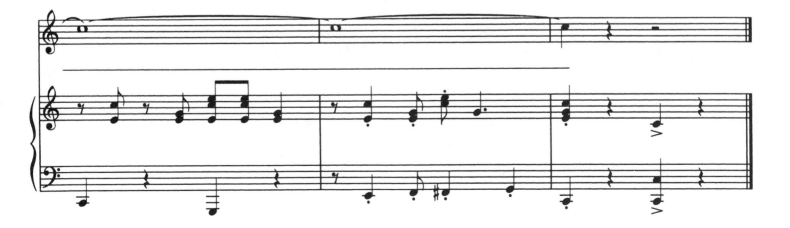

LORNA'S HERE
from GOLDEN BOY

Lyric by LEE ADAMS
Music by CHARLES STROUSE

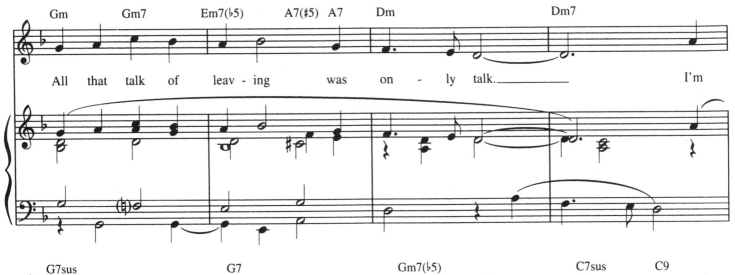

All that talk of leav-ing was on-ly talk.___ I'm

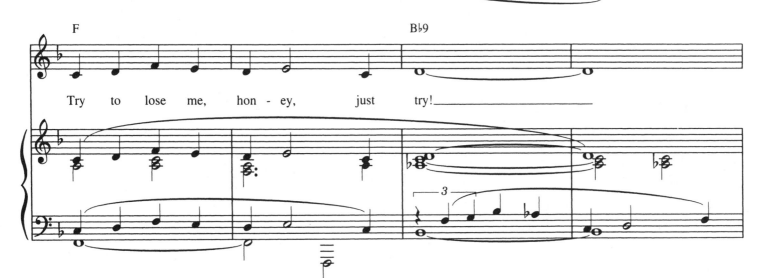

much too dumb___ to take that walk.___

Try to lose me, hon-ey, just try!___

Lor-na's here for-ev-er, you big ug-ly guy!___

MARRIED LIFE

from NICK AND NORA

Lyric by RICHARD MALTBY, JR.
Music by CHARLES STROUSE

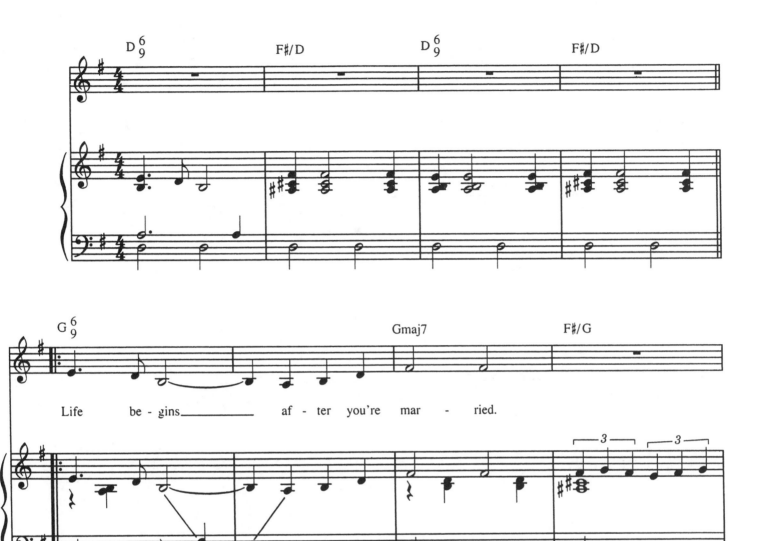

Life be - gins_____ af - ter you're mar - ried.

Who's to say_____ the way it starts?

A LOT OF LIVIN' TO DO
from BYE BYE BIRDIE

Lyric by LEE ADAMS
Music by CHARLES STROUSE

With a steady, growing drive

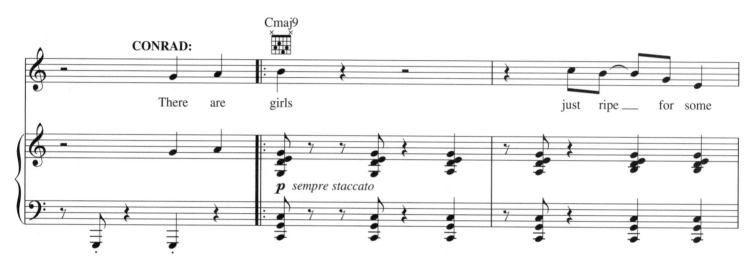

CONRAD:
There are girls just ripe ___ for some

kiss - in' ___ and I mean

to kiss ___ me a few! Oh, those

girls ... don't know _ what they're miss - in'. _

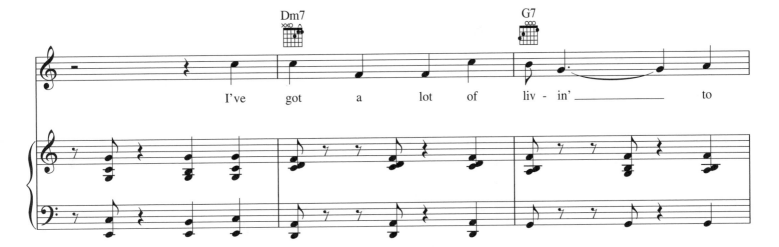

I've got a lot of liv - in' _____ to

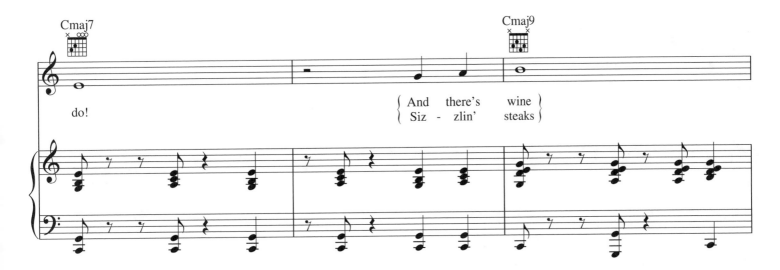

do!

{ And there's wine }
{ Siz - zlin' steaks }

all read - y for tast - in' ___ and there's

Cad - il - lacs all shin - y and new!

Got - ta move, 'cause time __ is a -

wast - in'. __ There's such a lot of

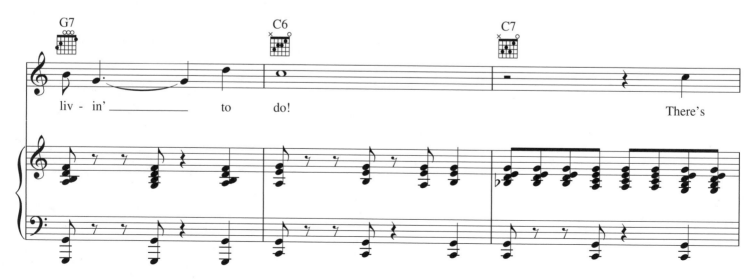

liv - in' _____ to do! There's

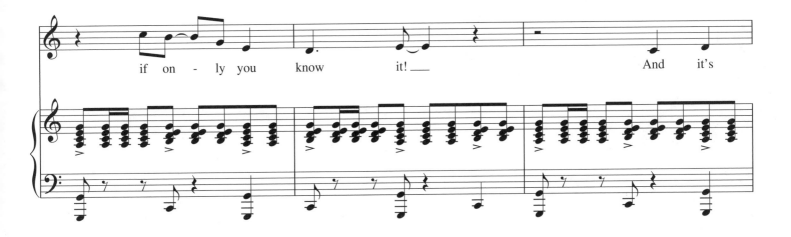

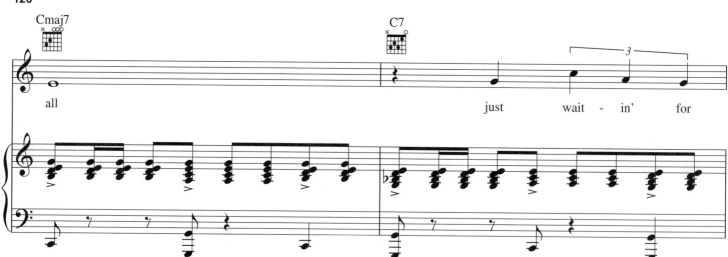

all ... just wait - in' for

you! ... You're a -

live, ... so come on and

show it! ___ ... There's

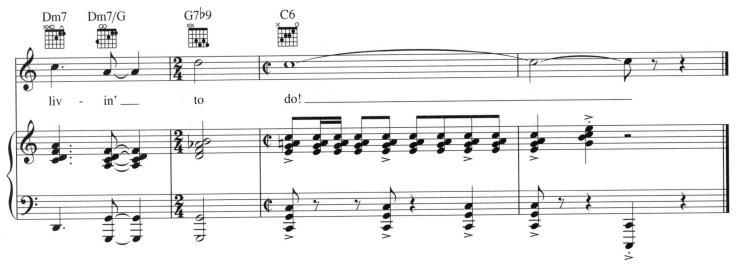

LOVE
from ANNIE WARBUCKS

Lyric by MARTIN CHARNIN
Music by CHARLES STROUSE

Moderately, in 2

Love ain't some-thin' you— can see, like

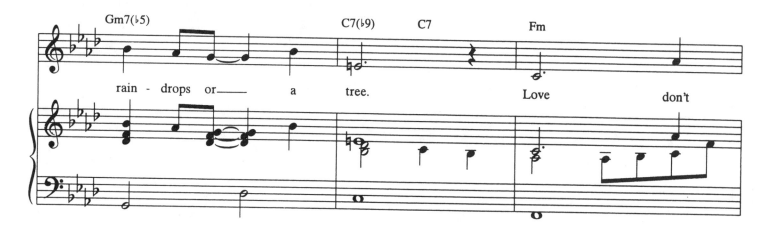

rain - drops or— a tree. Love don't

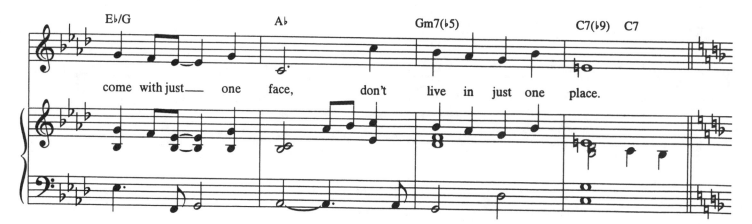

come with just— one face, don't live in just one place.

Gospel style (in 2)

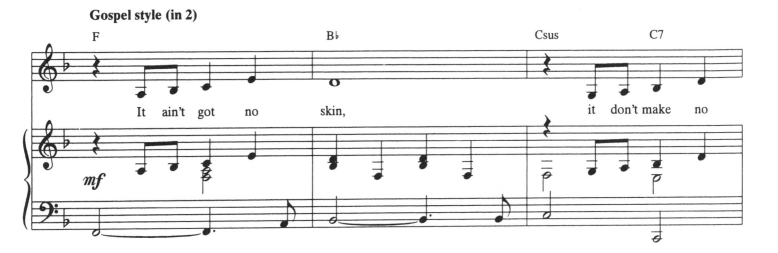

It ain't got no skin, it don't make no

sound. It just wig - gles in,

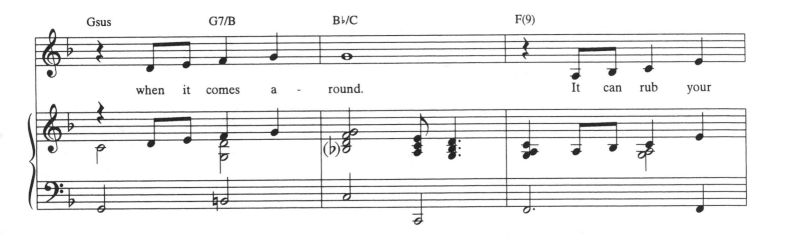

when it comes a - round. It can rub your

toes, e - ven comb your hair.

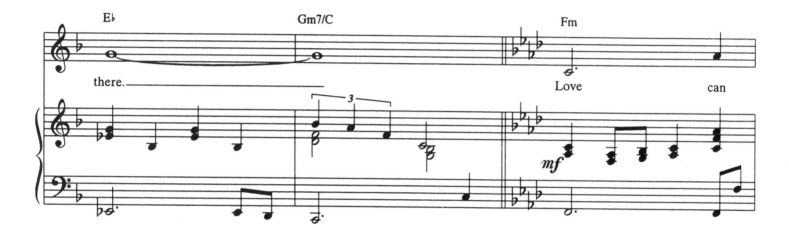

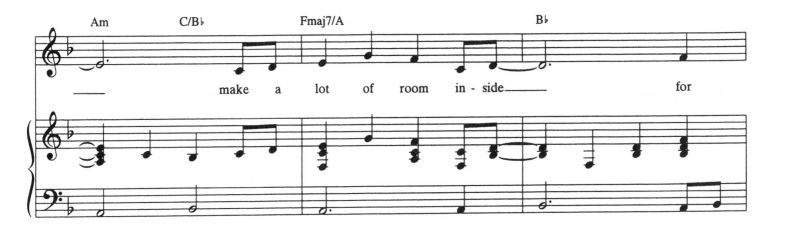

make a lot of room in-side_____ for

love, for love.

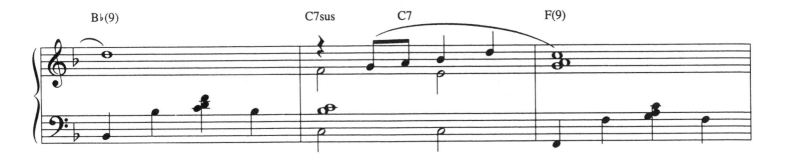

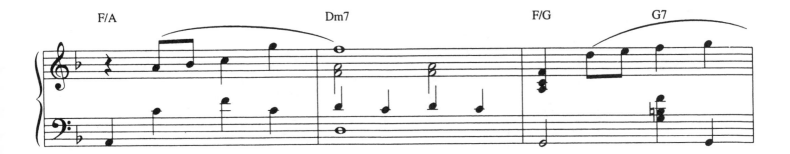

132

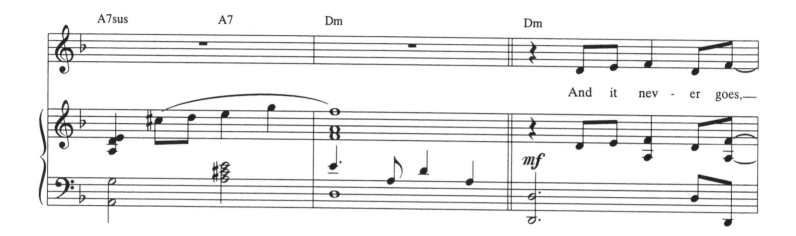

A♭   **Gm7(♭5)**   **C7(♭9)**   **C7**

cry,   but   those   are   tears   that   dry.

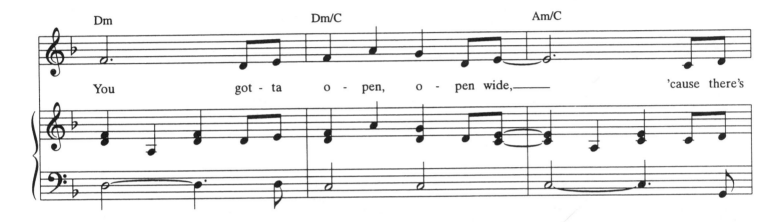

Dm   **Dm/C**   **Am/C**

You   got - ta   o - pen,   o - pen wide,_____   'cause there's

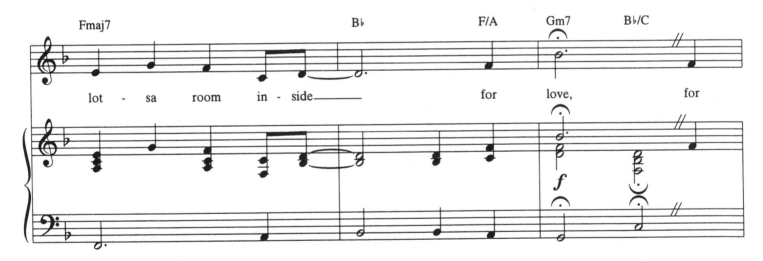

Fmaj7   **B♭**   **F/A**   **Gm7**   **B♭/C**

lot - sa   room   in - side_____   for   love,   for

f

B♭   **Am7**   **Gm7**   **E♭(9)**   **F**

love._____

MAYBE
from the Musical Production ANNIE

Lyric by MARTIN CHARNIN
Music by CHARLES STROUSE

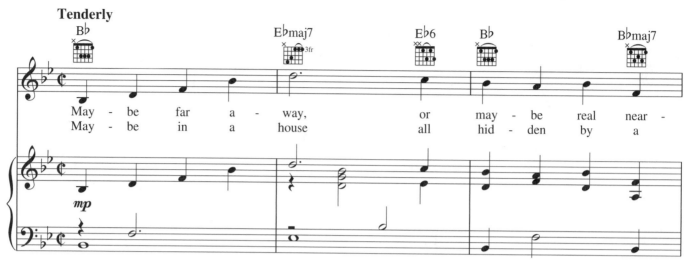

Tenderly

Maybe far a - way, or may - be real near -

Maybe in a house all hid - den by a

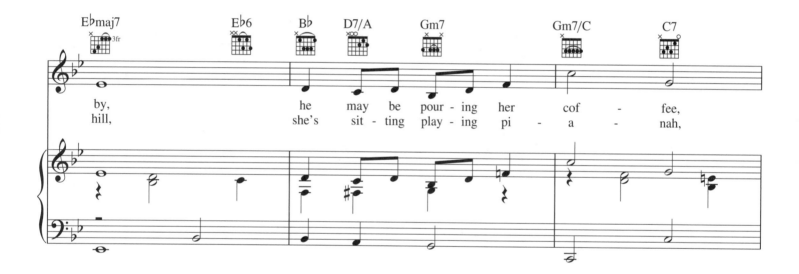

by, he may be pour - ing her cof - fee,

hill, she's sit - ting play - ing pi - a - nah,

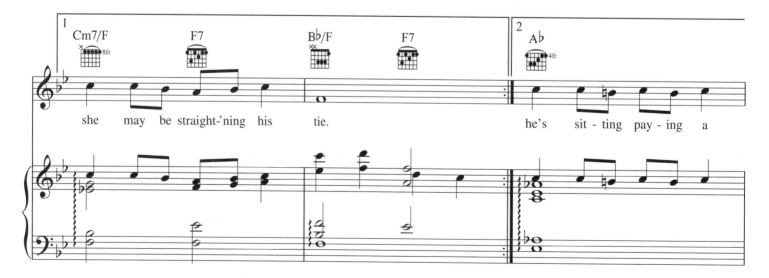

she may be straight-'ning his tie.

he's sit - ting pay - ing a

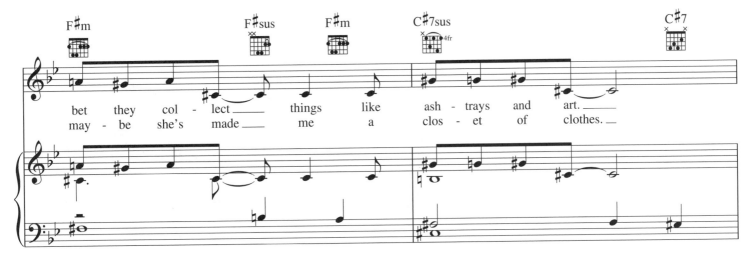

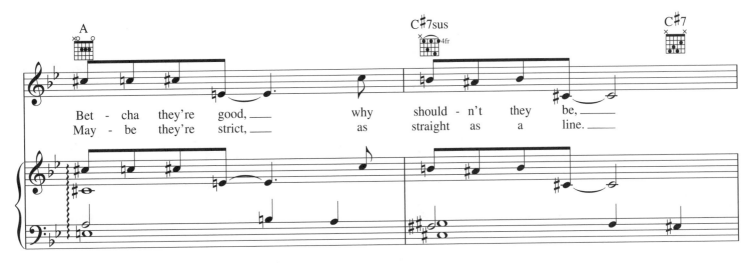

So, may - be now it's time, and
So, may - be now this prayer's the

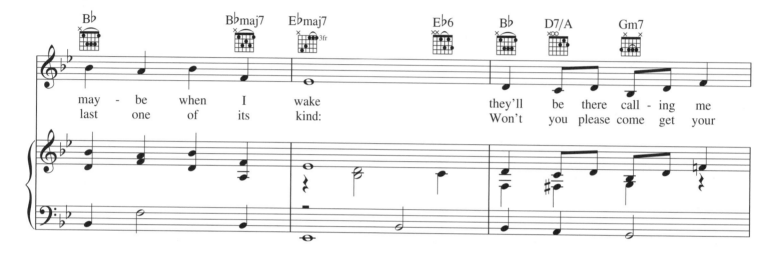

may - be when I wake
last one of its kind: they'll be there call - ing me
Won't you please come get your

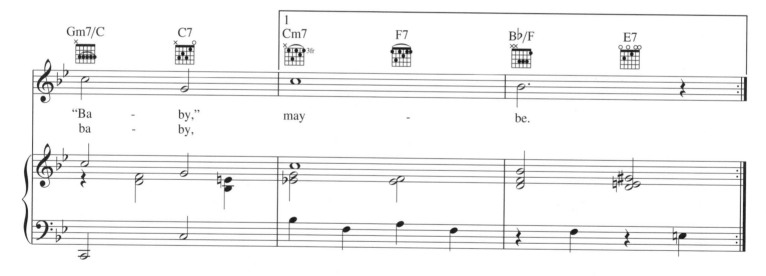

"Ba - by," may - be.
ba - by,

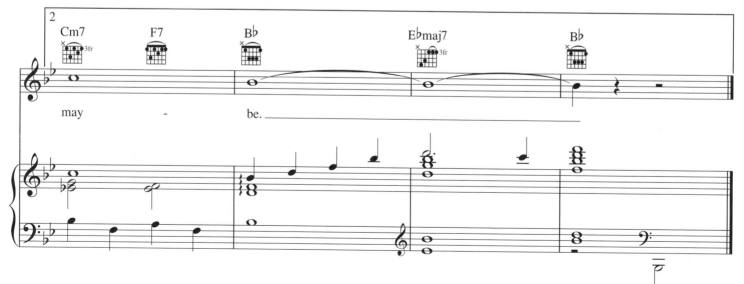

may - be. _____

MY STAR

from MARTY

Lyric by LEE ADAMS
Music by CHARLES STROUSE

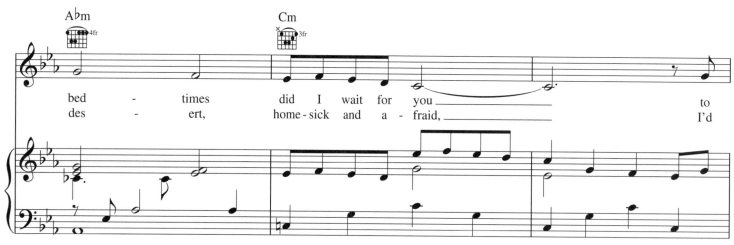

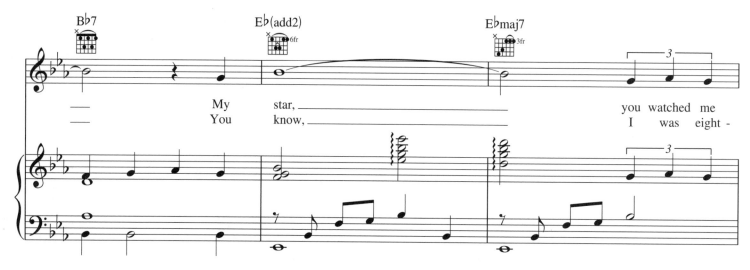

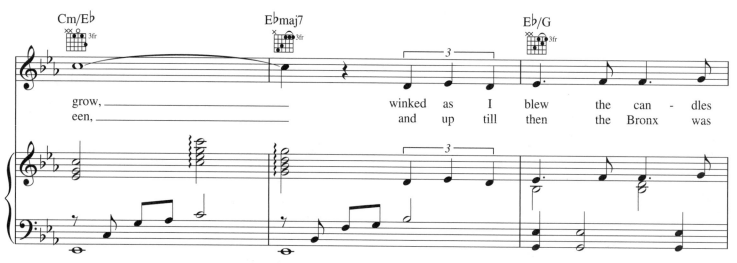

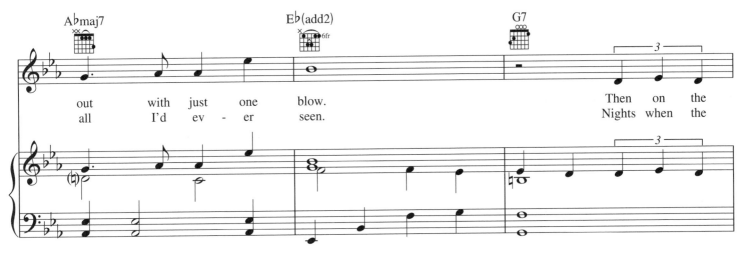

out with just one blow.
all I'd ev - er seen. Then on the
Nights when the

night that Pa - pa died, there you were watch - ing as I
shells burst all a - round, I'd say a prayer and hug the

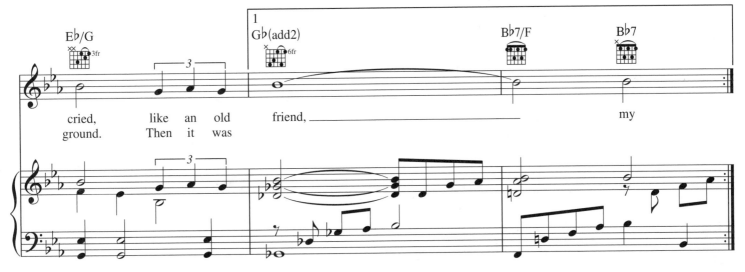

cried, like an old friend, my
ground. Then it was

there
like Pa - pa said it would be,

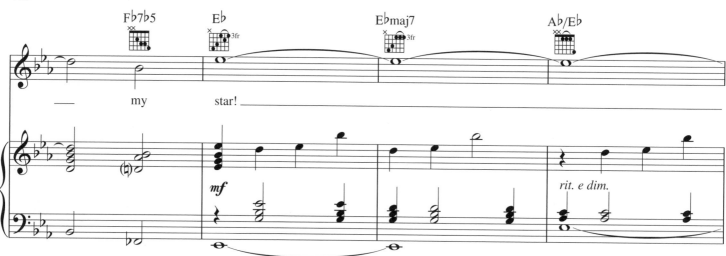

my star!

Freely

And so, my spe - cial star, you've al - ways been my faith - ful friend, and you still

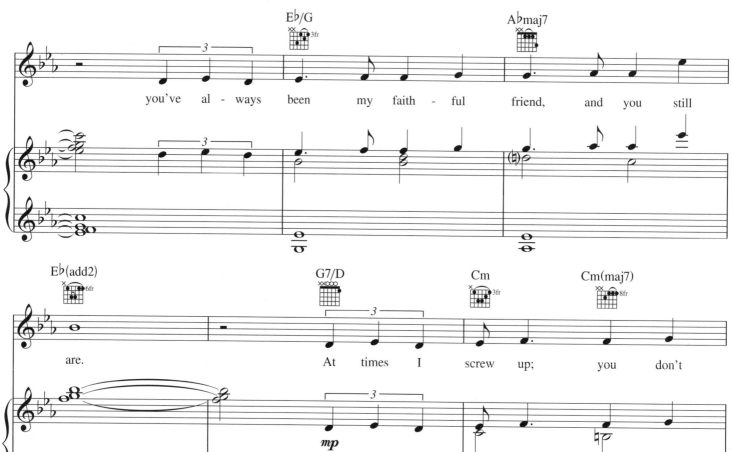

are. At times I screw up; you don't

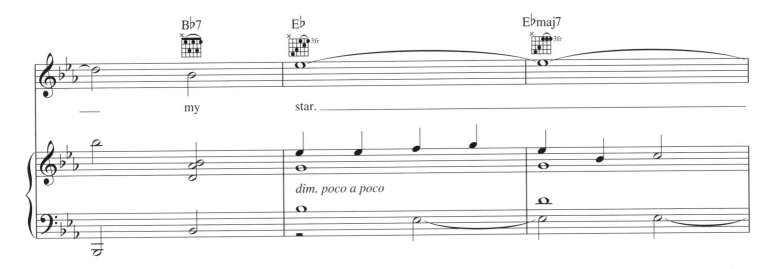

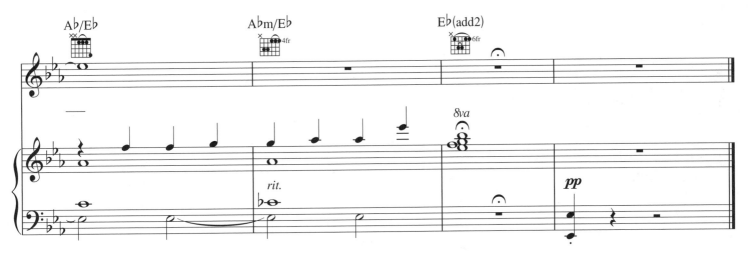

NIGHT SONG

from GOLDEN BOY

Lyric by LEE ADAMS
Music by CHARLES STROUSE

fro, _____ ev-'ry-one has some - one _____ and a place to

go. _____ Lis - ten, _____

hear the cars go past. _____ They don't e - ven

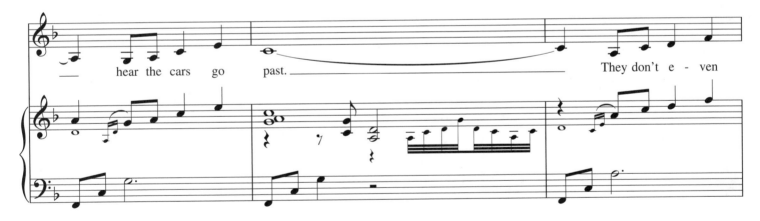

see me, _____ fly-ing by so fast; _____

don't e - ven know what it is you de - sire? _____
want to break out but your skin is your cage? _____

A little faster

Lis - ten. _____ Laugh - ter ev - 'ry - where! _____
Up - town— _____ just an - oth - er joe. _____

With mounting excitement

Hear it! _____ Life ___ is in the air! _____ As the
Down - town— _____ where ___ you gon - na go?... Al - ways

night comes _____ and the town a - wakes, _____ sound of chil - dren
Look - ing _____ for a place to be. _____ Where's the bright to -

N.Y.C.
from the Musical Production ANNIE

Lyric by MARTIN CHARNIN
Music by CHARLES STROUSE

N. Y. C., what is it a-bout you?
N. Y. C., the Hud-son at sun-down,

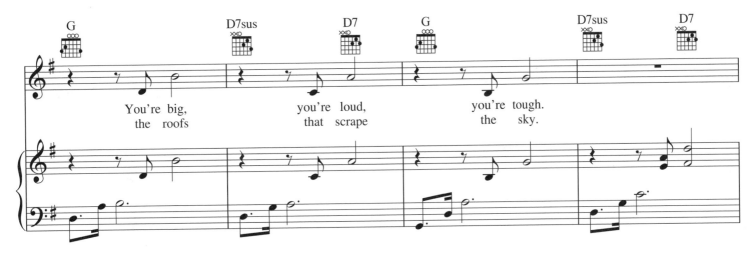

You're big, you're loud, you're tough.
the roofs that scrape the sky.

N. Y. C., I go years with-out you,
N. Y. C., the rich and the run-down,

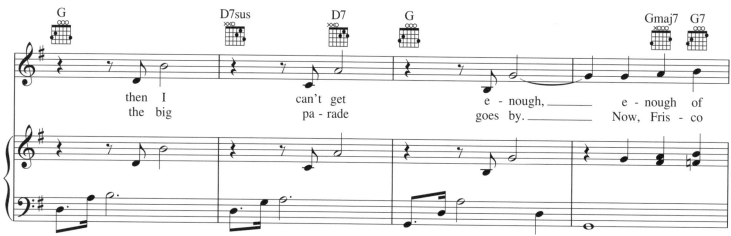

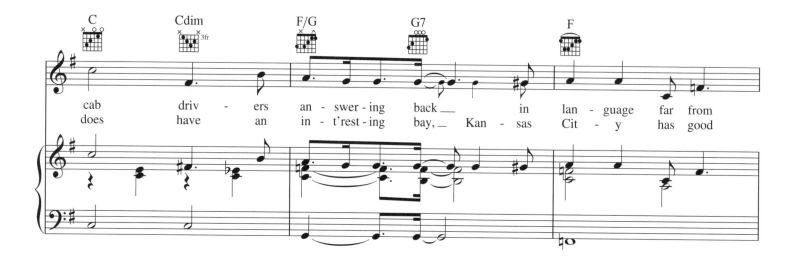

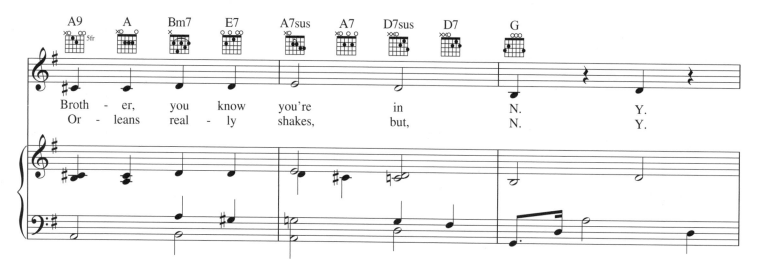

too bus - y, too cra - zy,
you make 'em all post - cards.

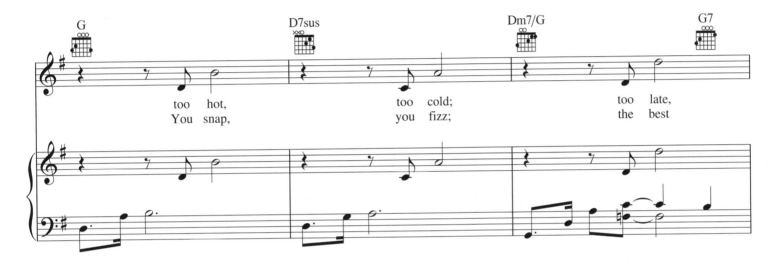

too hot, too cold; too late,
You snap, you fizz; the best

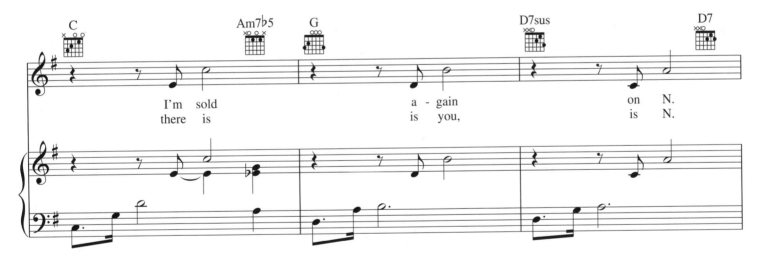

I'm sold a - gain on N.
there is is you, is N.

Y. C.
Y. C.

NO MAN IS WORTH IT

from DANCE A LITTLE CLOSER

Lyric by ALAN JAY LERNER
Music by CHARLES STROUSE

1. No man is worth all the lows you get_____ from the highs you get from a man.
2. No man is worth all the burns you get_____ from the flame you get from a man.

No man is worth all the hopes you get_____ from the
No man is worth all the fun you get_____ from the

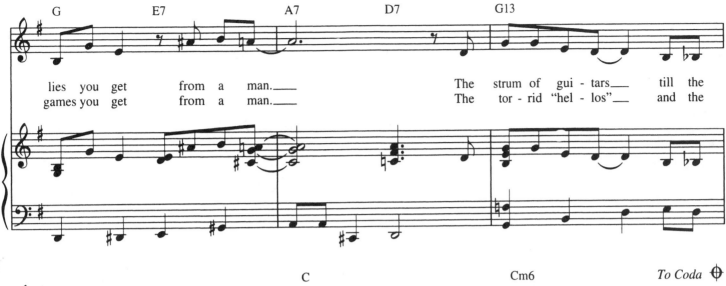

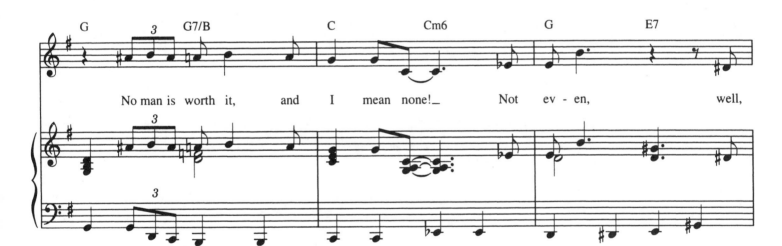

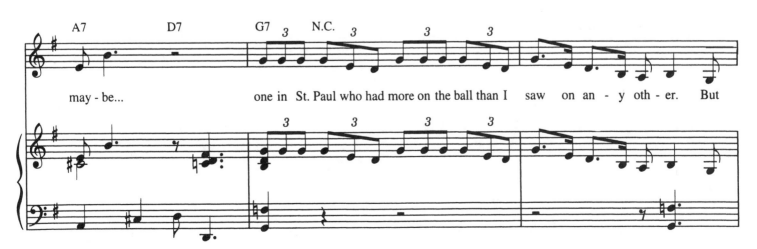

ONCE UPON A TIME
from the Broadway Musical ALL AMERICAN

Lyric by LEE ADAMS
Music by CHARLES STROUSE

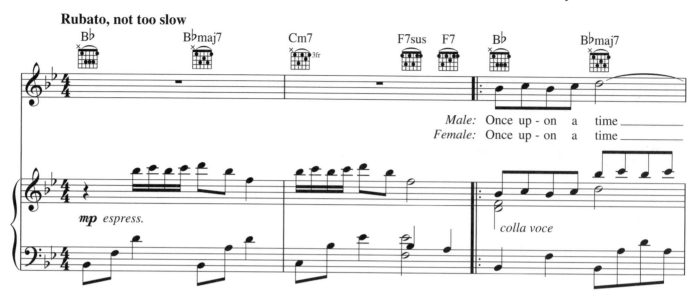

But that was once up-on a time, _____ ver-y long a-
The world was beau-ti-ful to see _____ ver-y long a-

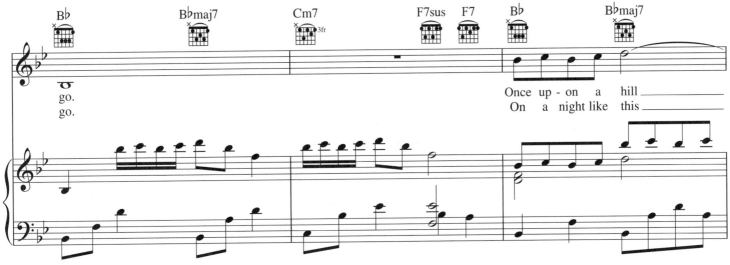

go.
go.

Once up-on a hill _____
On a night like this _____

___ we sat be - neath a wil-low tree, _____
___ we saw the ris - ing of the moon. _____

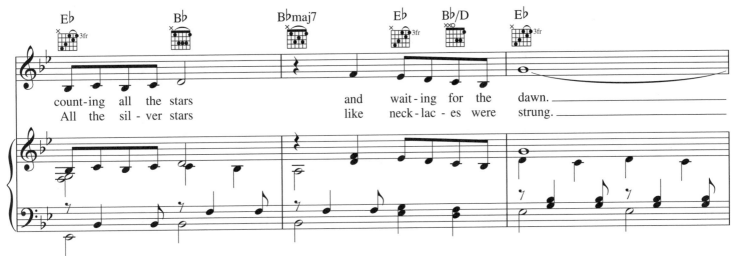

count-ing all the stars and wait-ing for the dawn. _____
All the sil-ver stars like neck-lac-es were strung. _____

But that was once up-on a time. _____ Now the tree is
We spoke of such im-por-tant things. _____ We were ver-y

gone.
young.
How the breeze
O - pen hearts,

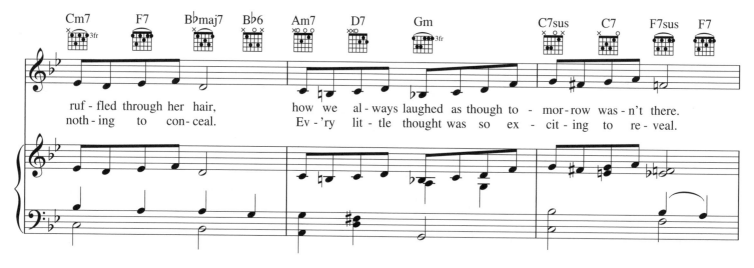

ruf - fled through her hair, how we al-ways laughed as though to-mor-row was-n't there.
noth-ing to con-ceal. Ev-'ry lit-tle thought was so ex-cit-ing to re-veal.

We were young and did - n't have a care. Where did it go?
All our dreams we knew would soon be real. Where did they go?

poco rit.

Tempo I

ONE BOY (GIRL)

from BYE BYE BIRDIE

Lyric by LEE ADAMS
Music by CHARLES STROUSE

one cer - tain {boy.} {girl.} One {boy} {girl} to laugh with, to joke with, have Coke with.

One {boy, _____} {girl, _____} not two, or three. _____

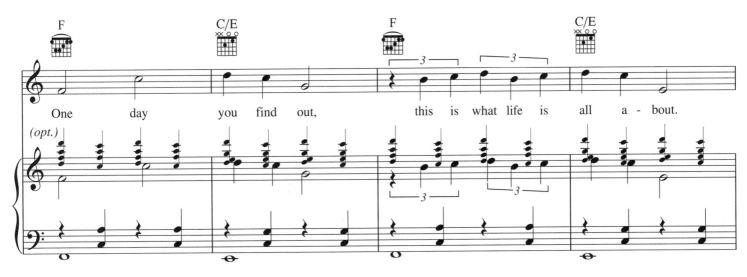

One day you find out, this is what life is all a - bout.

(opt.)

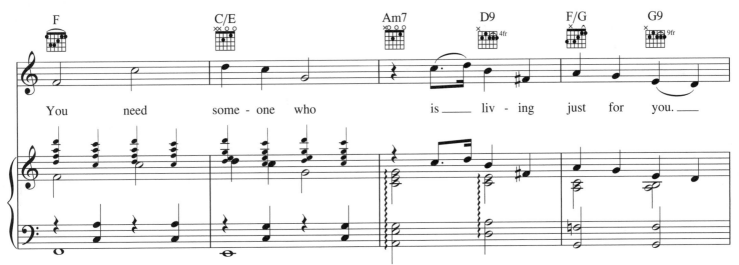

You need some - one who is ___ liv - ing just for you. ___

PALS
from LYLE THE CROCODILE

Words and Music by
CHARLES STROUSE

PUT ON A HAPPY FACE

from BYE BYE BIRDIE

Lyric by LEE ADAMS
Music by CHARLES STROUSE

SATURDAY NIGHT GIRL
from MARTY

Lyric by LEE ADAMS
Music by CHARLES STROUSE

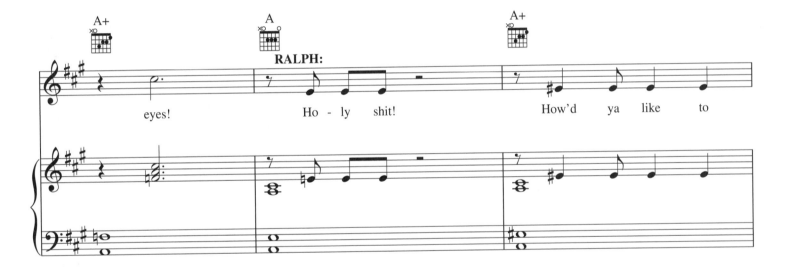

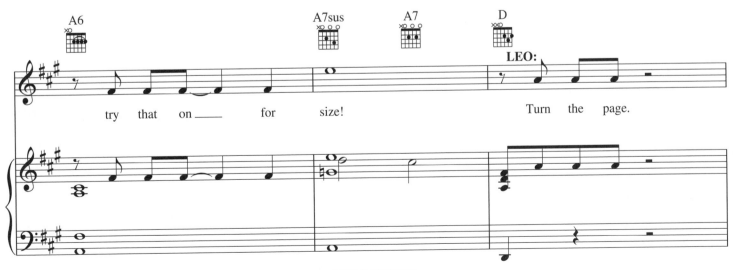

ho-ur is late and she's wait-in', my Sat-ur-day night girl.___

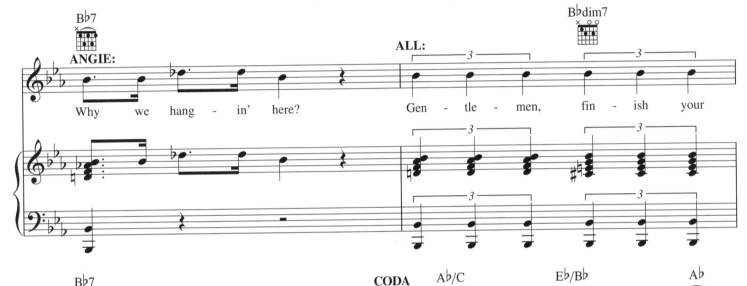

ANGIE: Why we hang-in' here? **ALL:** Gen-tle-men, fin-ish your

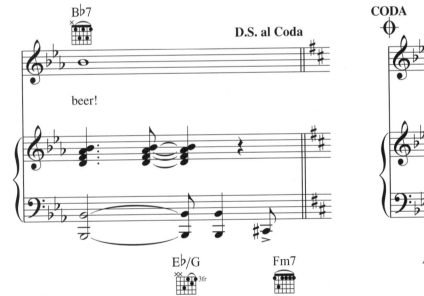

beer!

D.S. al Coda

CODA Look out, it's Sat-ur-day, watch___

___ out, it's Sat-ur-day, ooh,___ ooh, it's Sat-ur-day night!___

SMASHING, NEW YORK TIMES
from APPLAUSE

Lyric by LEE ADAMS
Music by CHARLES STROUSE

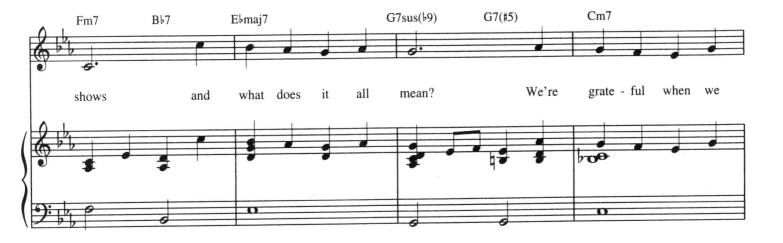

shows and what does it all mean? We're grate - ful when we

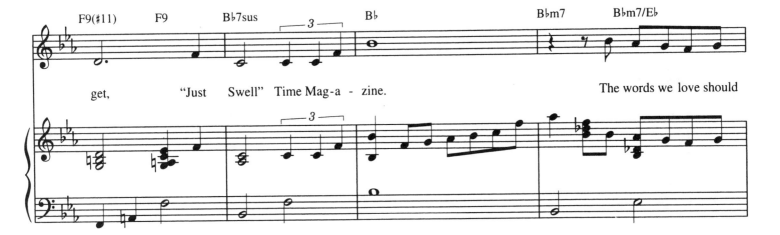

get, "Just Swell" Time Mag-a - zine. The words we love should

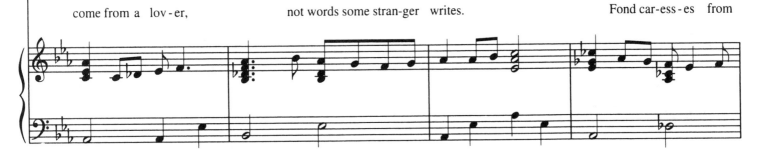

come from a lov - er, not words some stran-ger writes. Fond car-ess - es from

news - pa - per press-es won't warm you on win-ter nights. Well, dop - ey

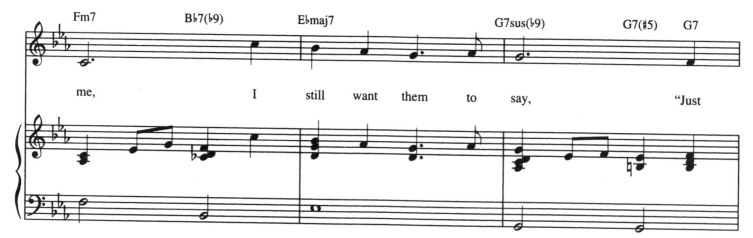

me,   I   still   want   them   to   say,   "Just

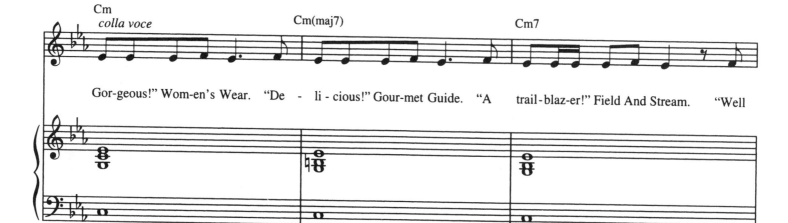

Gor-geous!" Wom-en's Wear. "De - li - cious!" Gour-met Guide. "A   trail-blaz-er!" Field And Stream.   "Well

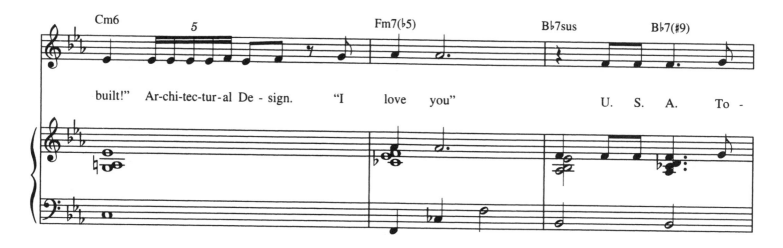

built!" Ar-chi-tec-tur-al De - sign.   "I   love   you"   U. S. A. To-

day._____

THIS IS THE LIFE
from GOLDEN BOY

Lyric by LEE ADAMS
Music by CHARLES STROUSE

Brightly

This Is___ The Life!   Here's where___ the liv-in' is!
This Is___ The Life!   Here's where___ it's hap-pen - ing!

This Is___ The Life!   Ba - by,___ we're there!
This Is___ The Life!   We're on___ our way!

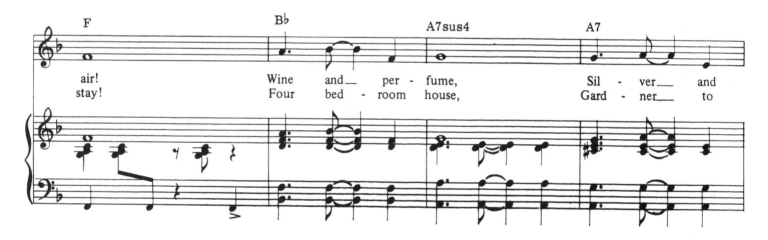

free! }
long! }

Noth - ing but class

That's how it's gon - na be!_____ This Is The

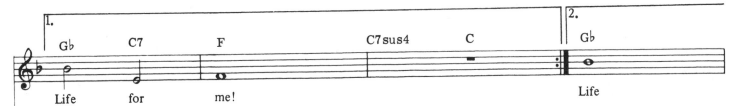

1.
Gb   C7   F   C7sus4   C   2. Gb
Life   for   me!   Life

C   F   Cm7   F   Cm7   F
for   me!_____

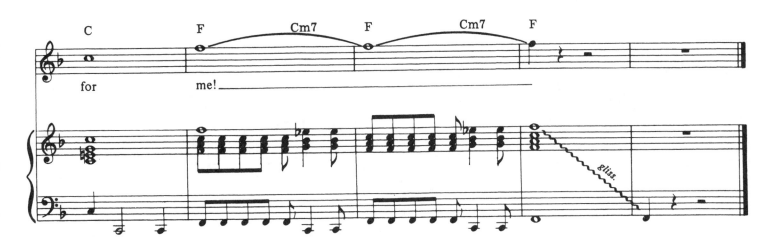

There's Always One You Can't Forget

from DANCE A LITTLE CLOSER

Lyric by ALAN JAY LERNER
Music by CHARLES STROUSE

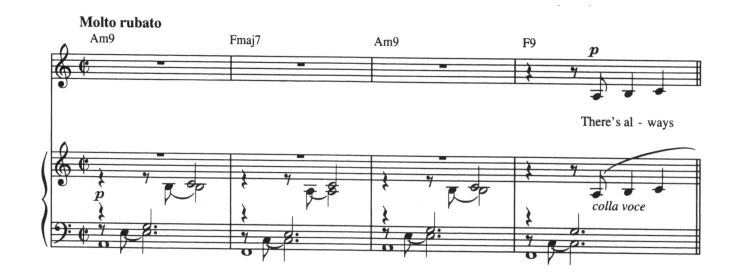

THERE'S NEVER BEEN ANYTHING LIKE US

from DANCE A LITTLE CLOSER

Lyric by ALAN JAY LERNER
Music by CHARLES STROUSE

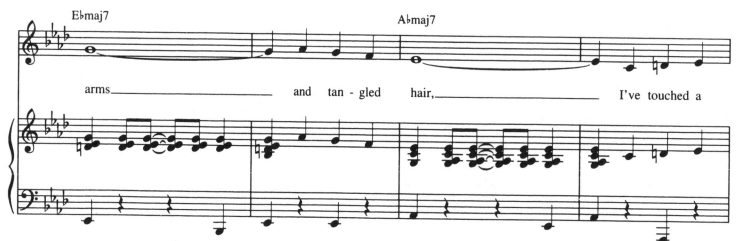

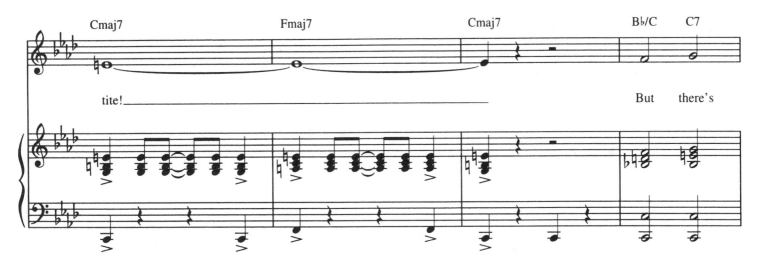

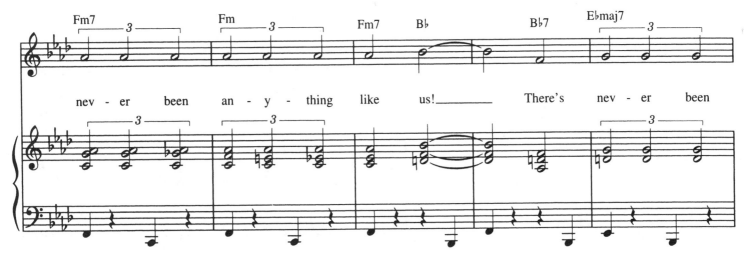

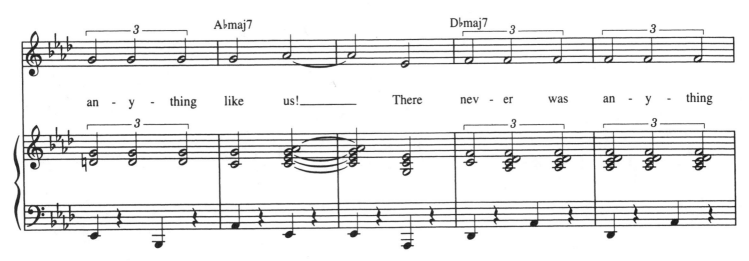

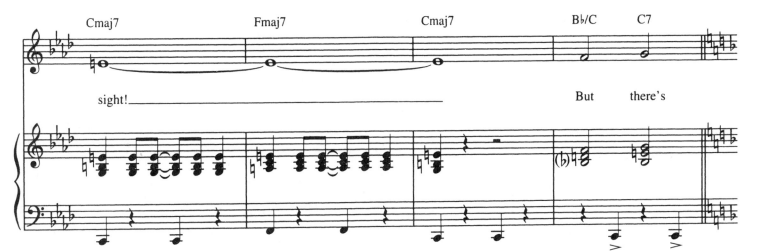

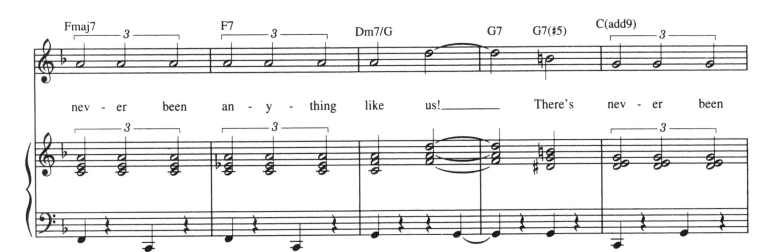

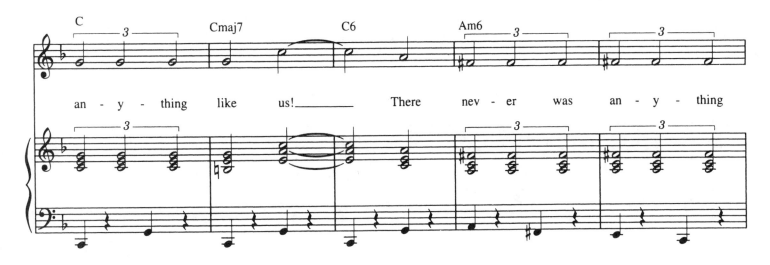

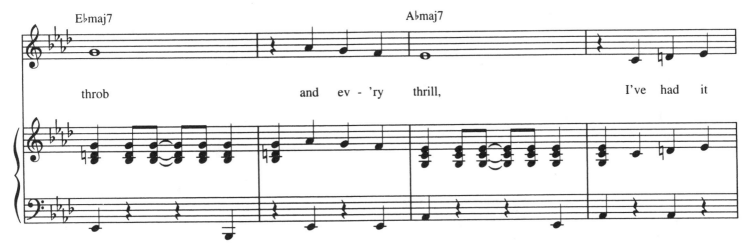

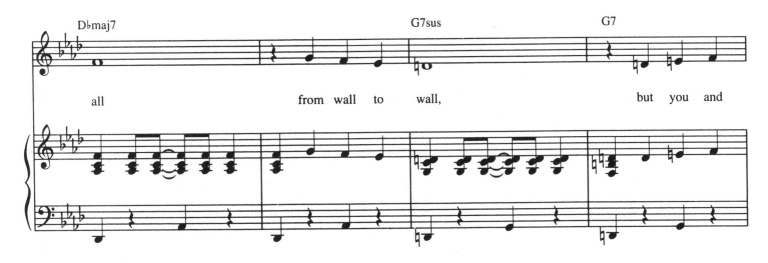

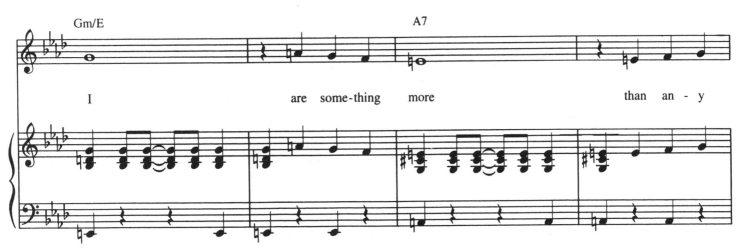

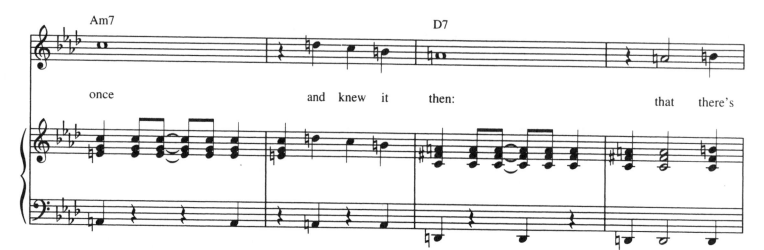

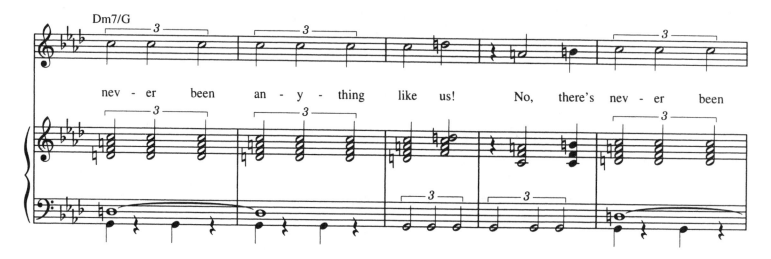

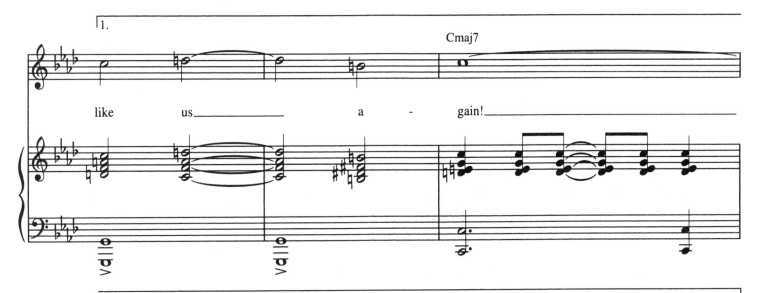

like us_____ a - gain!_____

like us_____ a -

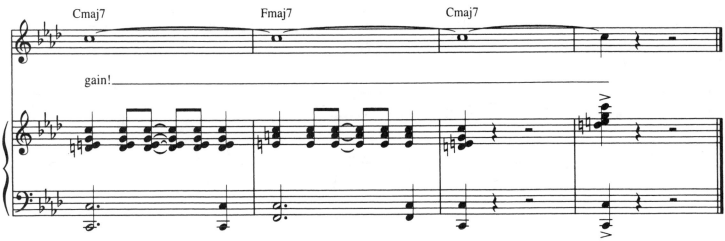

gain!_____

191

THOSE WERE THE DAYS
TV Theme from ALL IN THE FAMILY

Music by CHARLES STROUSE
Words by LEE ADAMS

WANTING
from RAGS

Lyric by STEPHEN SCHWARTZ
Music by CHARLES STROUSE

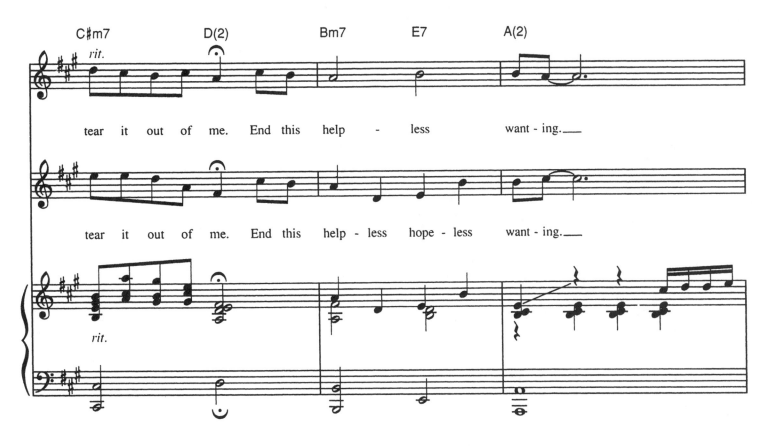

tear it out of me. End this help - less want - ing.___

tear it out of me. End this help - less hope - less want - ing.___

Both:

Don't I ev-er learn? No, I stand here want -

Tempo I

ing.

TOMORROW

from the Musical Production ANNIE

Lyric by MARTIN CHARNIN
Music by CHARLES STROUSE

Lyrics:
The sun-'ll come out ____ to-mor-row, bet your bot-tom dol-lar that to-mor-row ____ there'll be sun! Jus' think-ing a-bout ____ to-mor-row

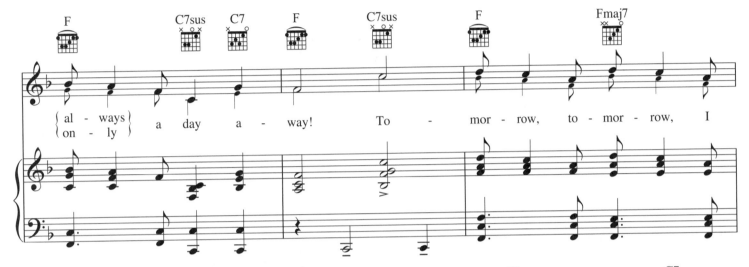

WHAT AM I GONNA DO WITHOUT YOU?

from the new GOLDEN BOY

Lyric by LEE ADAMS
Music by CHARLES STROUSE

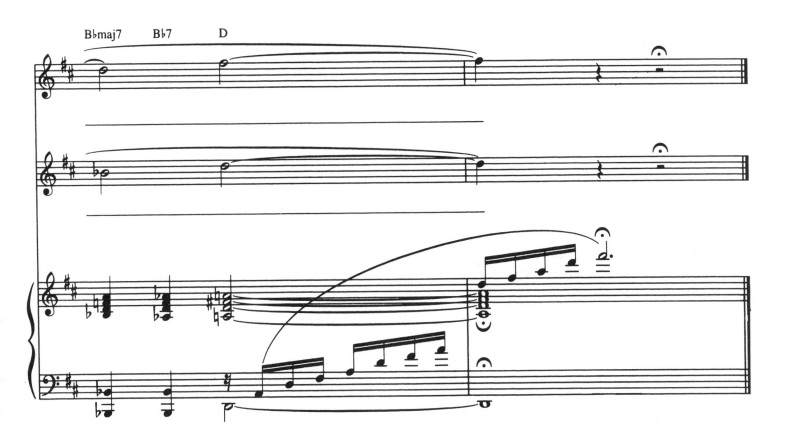

WHEN YOU SMILE

from ANNIE WARBUCKS

Lyric by MARTIN CHARNIN
Music by CHARLES STROUSE

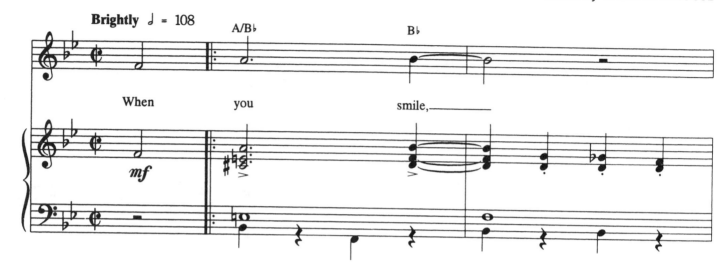

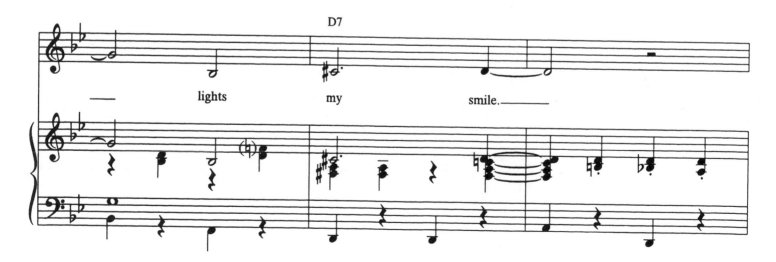

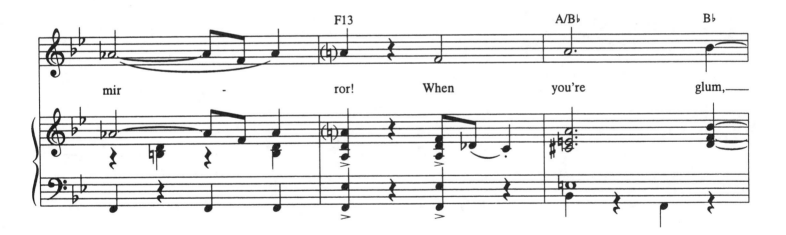

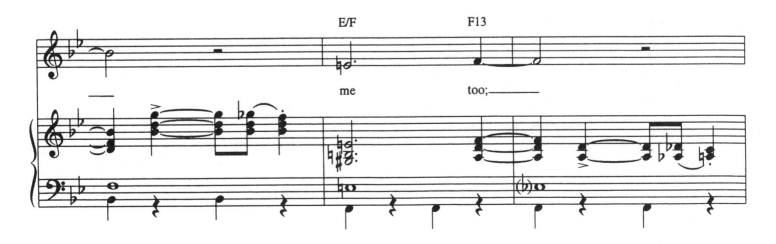

I'm all_____ at sea too!_____

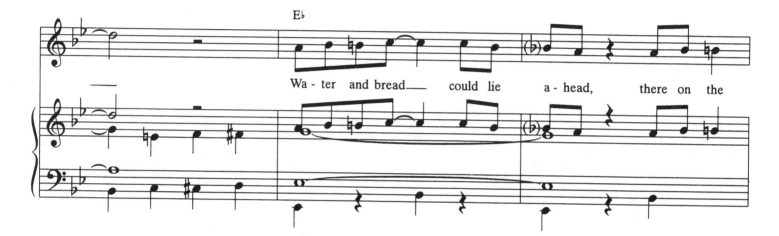

Wa- ter and bread_____ could lie a- head, there on the

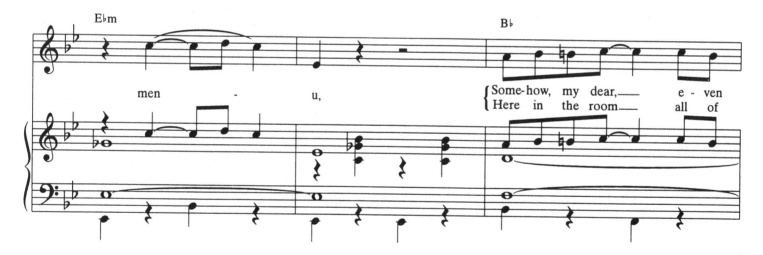

men - u,

Some-how, my dear,____ e - ven
Here in the room____ all of

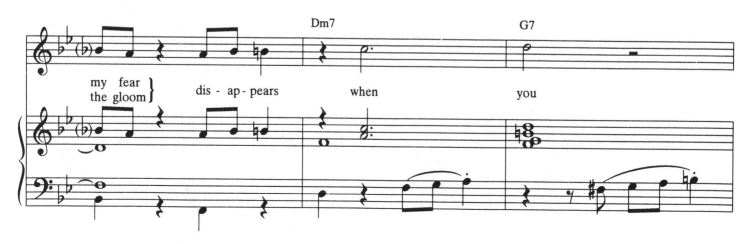

my fear
the gloom } dis - ap - pears when you

flash that_____ great big_____ gor - geous smile.

When gor - geous_____

smile._____

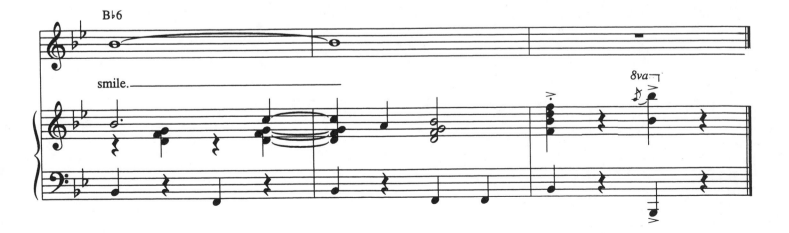

YOU'RE NEVER FULLY DRESSED WITHOUT A SMILE

from the Musical Production ANNIE

Lyric by MARTIN CHARNIN
Music by CHARLES STROUSE

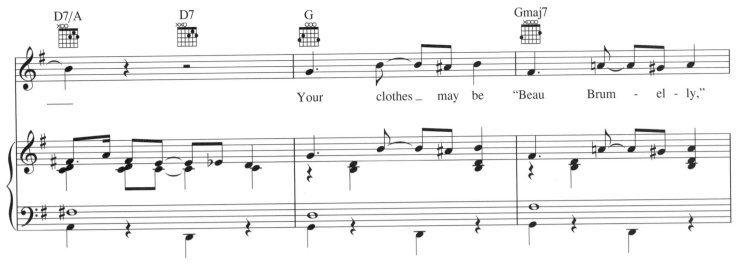

Your clothes _ may be "Beau Brum - el - ly,"

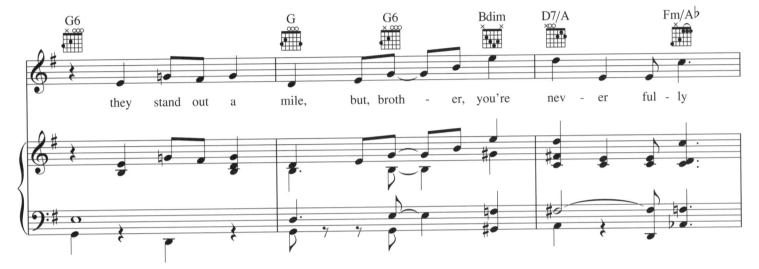

they stand out a mile, but, broth - er, you're nev - er ful - ly

dressed with - out a smile! _____ Who

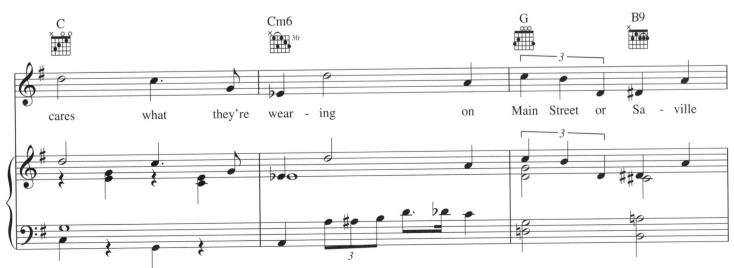

cares what they're wear - ing on Main Street or Sa - ville

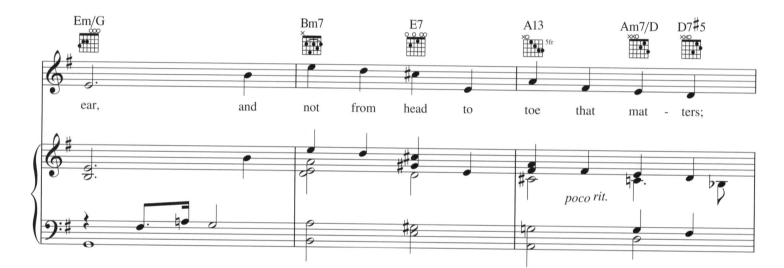

YOU'VE GOT POSSIBILITIES

from IT'S A BIRD, IT'S A PLANE, IT'S SUPERMAN

Lyric by LEE ADAMS
Music by CHARLES STROUSE

pos - si - bil - i - ties. Let me__ pry__ you from your shell!

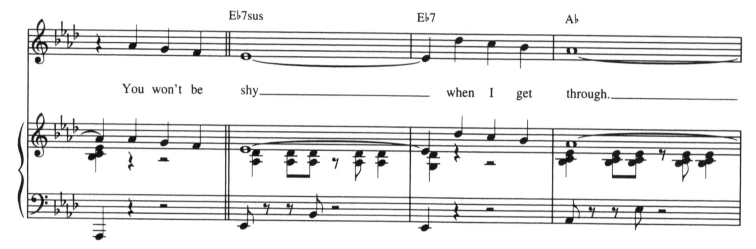

You won't be shy_____ when I get through._____

__ Come on and roar,_____ you ti - ger you!

Some - where__ 'way down deep__ in you, there's life,__ no doubt!

It's just___ been a-sleep___ in you. Let me___ bring it out.___ Yes,

you've got___ pos-si-bil-i-ties. May-be e-ven a lot!

Red hot___ pos-si-bil-i-ties you don't___ e-ven know

you've got!___

WHATEVER TIME THERE IS
from FLOWERS FOR ALGERNON

Lyric by DAVID ROGERS
Music by CHARLES STROUSE

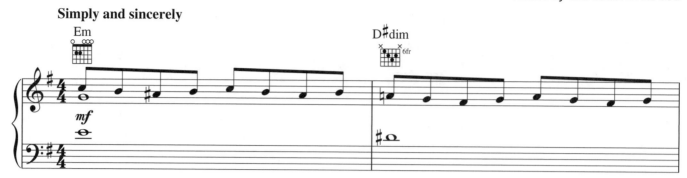

What - ev - er time there is, a mil - lion days or

two, I want to spend them all with you. What - ev - er time there

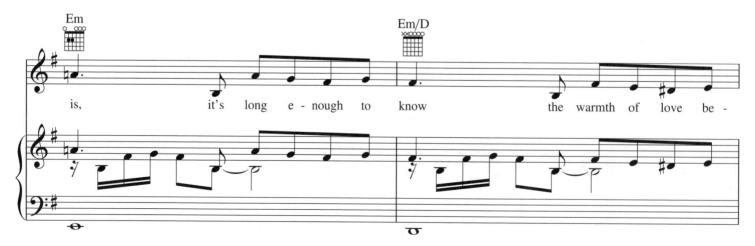

is, it's long e - nough to know the warmth of love be -

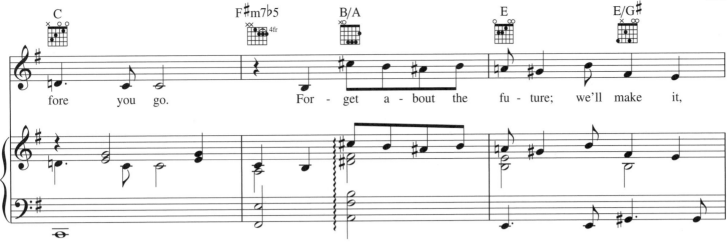

-fore you go. For - get a - bout the fu - ture; we'll make it,

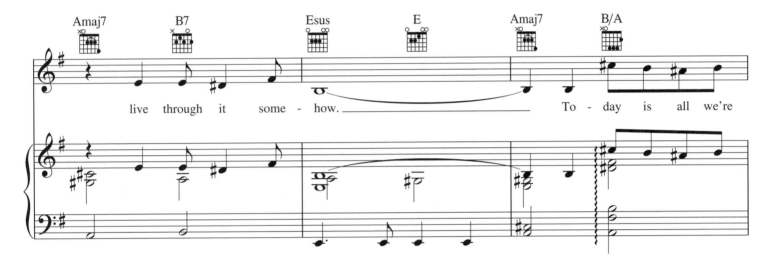

live through it some - how. _____ To - day is all we're

giv - en; let's take it, live our whole lives now! _____

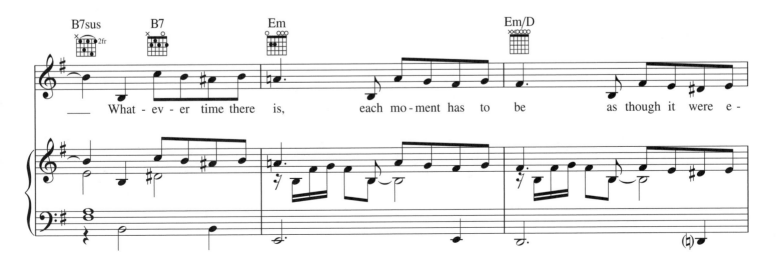

____ What - ev - er time there is, each mo - ment has to be as though it were e-

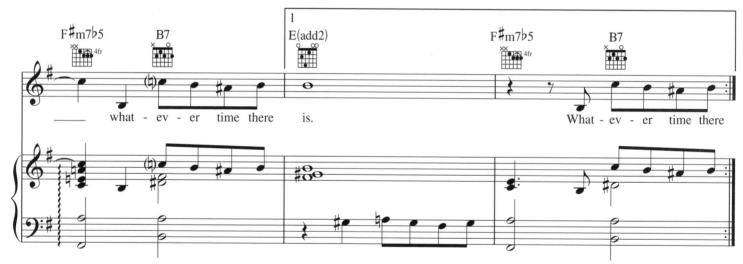

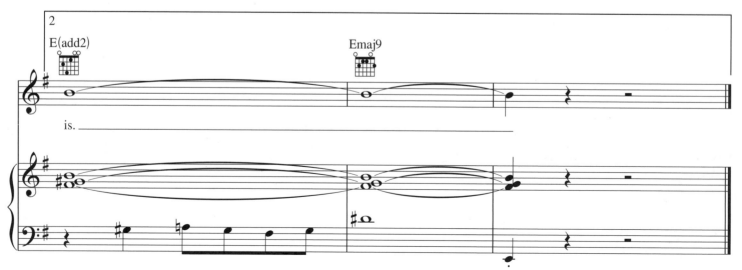